ORDINARY
WOMEN
EXTRAORDINARY
WISDOM

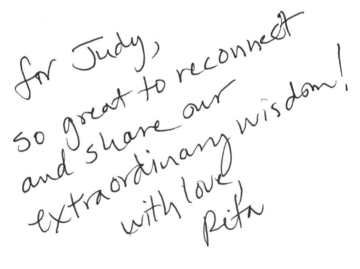

for Judy,
so great to reconnect
and share our
extraordinary wisdom!
with love
Rita

Winchester, UK
Washington, USA

First published by O Books, 2007
O Books is an imprint of John Hunt Publishing Ltd.,
The Bothy, Deershot Lodge, Park Lane, Ropley, Hants, SO24 0BE, UK
office1@o-books.net
www.o-books.net

Distribution in:

UK and Europe
Orca Book Services
orders@orcabookservices.co.uk
Tel: 01202 665432 Fax: 01202 666219 Int. code (44)

USA and Canada
NBN
custserv@nbnbooks.com
Tel: 1 800 462 6420 Fax: 1 800 338 4550

Australia and New Zealand
Brumby Books
sales@brumbybooks.com.au
Tel: 61 3 9761 5535 Fax: 61 3 9761 7095

Far East (offices in Singapore, Thailand, Hong Kong, Taiwan)
Pansing Distribution Pte Ltd
kemal@pansing.com
Tel: 65 6319 9939 Fax: 65 6462 5761

South Africa
Alternative Books
altbook@peterhyde.co.za
Tel: 021 447 5300 Fax: 021 447 1430

Text copyright © Rita Robinson 2007

Design: Stuart Davies

ISBN: 978 1 84694 068 2

A CIP catalogue record for this book is available from the British Library.

Printed in the US by Maple Vail

ORDINARY WOMEN EXTRAORDINARY WISDOM

The Feminine Face of Awakening

Rita Marie Robinson

BOOKS

Winchester, UK
Washington, USA

ACKNOWLEDGEMENTS

The writing of this book represents a culmination of my entire life's walk, a journey shaped by many people, many gifts. I take this moment to raise my glass to celebrate and honor each of you.

First, to Mom and Dad, Jan and Richard, who planted the seeds of unlimited potential and taught me to never question my value as a woman. To my former husband, Brian Rapp, whose death initiated me into the depths of love and the reality of impermanence. To my loving partner and ultimate "teacher" Chris Bowles, who challenges me to "walk the talk" in daily life. To my spiritual sister, Ulli Sir Jesse, a dear companion on this unfolding path. To my Girl Scout buddies, Janis Rutschman and Vickie Sewing, whose warm friendship made Santa Fe home, fertile ground for the birthing of this book. To the wise women in my Sacred Circle, where the power and the potential of the feminine is embodied. To my colleagues, my cheerleaders, my critics: Connie Anderson, Amy Cannon, Carol Dix, Nan Dudek, Leigh Fortson, Linda Hoeksema, Karen Kinnett Hyatt, Peggy Kappy, Becky Strouse and Rosemerry Wahtolla Trommer. And to my beloved land, Flying Hawks, where I am nurtured by earth and sky, the silence, the wildness, and the Source of all.

Finally, let me express my gratitude to all the women that I interviewed. I thank you for your openness, your loving presence, and your insistence on our sameness. To Jeannie Zandi, thank you for the subtitle. And to Pamela Wilson, thank you for your friendship, the most precious gift of all.

To the nameless mystery that moved through me from the moment the idea was born to the writing of each and every word... there is no way to express my gratitude, my awe, my humility.

CONTENTS

DEDICATION

To the mystery,
the wisdom,
and the love
at the heart of
each and every one of us

ABOUT THE AUTHOR

Like many of her generation, Rita Marie Robinson has been on a lifelong search. Innocently looking outside of herself for the answer, she explored many paths—the occult, shamanism, Buddhism and New Thought Churches. Her work interests were equally eclectic—she worked as a radio journalist, in real estate sales and development, and finally as a psychotherapist. She received her Masters Degree in 1995 from Pacifica Graduate Institute, known for its archetypal and soul-centered approach to counseling. After the death of her husband in 1994, Rita trained as a hospice volunteer and in Joan Halifax's program, "Compassionate Care of the Dying." Rita has lived and worked in Santa Barbara, Santa Fe and Telluride, Colorado where she currently lives on a peaceful mountaintop with her longtime partner, Chris, along with their dog, and a big garden.

INTRODUCTION

I was 14 years old when I first realized that there was something more to life than growing up and having the perfect family. A friend and I were bored and hungry for life to start, but we were in that awkward limbo—too old and not old enough. We had read somewhere about fasting and decided that sounded interesting, so we stopped eating. After 24 hours without food, we were feeling a little light-headed. We turned off the lights in her bedroom and looked out the window of her middle-class house in the suburbs. It was like seeing the stars for the first time.

Maybe the lack of food stopped my mind's normal functioning for a moment, who knows. But I let it all in, the infinite vastness of the universe. I fully felt the reality that each star was a sun, and each sun had its own planets and moons all spinning within a solar system, within a galaxy, with other galaxies, on and on until my mind just gave up trying to grasp infinity. This is it, I thought. This is the mystery and wonder which all the great religions point to. It was in that moment that the longing was born. I had no idea what I was longing for, but I was now aware of a sense of emptiness, a wanting and a waiting for fulfillment.

That longing sparked a lifelong search that pushed me from one spiritual path to another. And eventually lead to the abandonment of the search in favor of more attainable goals, like building a house and a good career. Years later, after the death of my husband and a lot of other dead ends, I found myself searching again. I moved from the mountains of Colorado to Santa Fe, leaving behind my partner Chris, my work as a psychotherapist and all that I had created in my home of 20 years.

It was at a *The Power of Now* workshop with Karen McPhee that I was introduced to what I now call the *direct path*. I had read *The Power of Now*, but a book is no substitute for the actual experience of stillness itself. I was deeply touched so I asked someone if anyone local offered the same simple approach and was directed to a woman in the audience. I couldn't believe it. She looked so normal—flannel shirt, jeans, long blonde hair, in her mid-40s. "Yes, that's Pamela Wilson."

I saw Pamela one evening the next week at a gathering called *satsang*. I'd never heard that word before. *Satsang* originates from Sanskrit and means "being together in truth." I learned that *satsang* is a chance to rest from all seeking and longing and just appreciate the mystery of who we are. There is no hierarchy, no concepts or rituals; only the experience of your true nature in the here-and-now. This is the definition of the *direct path of awakening*.

At the beginning of Pamela's *satsang*, there was a half hour of silence. Then Pamela opened her sparkly eyes, bowed and said with an impish grin, "Welcome to *satsang*." People asked questions or explored issues as Pamela used a process of Self-inquiry, "Who is having this problem? What is aware of this feeling?" Pamela's invitation to look within often ended in a moment of silence, maybe a smile or a sigh, the recognition of something indescribable. It was obvious that there were no words that could answer the perennial question, "Who am I?"

Pamela didn't explain much about all this. She did mention that she had been influenced by a Western teacher, Robert Adams. His death was a catalyst for her to get serious about her "recognition" which Pamela describes as the realization of one's true nature. Pamela uses the word recognition instead of enlightenment so the mind doesn't try to make a big deal out of it.

I had never heard of Robert Adams and went to the local bookstore to try and put the pieces together. I learned Robert Adams was a disciple of Ramana Maharshi, an Indian sage who used Self-inquiry to point people toward the truth of their being. He brought to life the ancient Hindu teachings of "non-duality" known as Advaita. Simply put, "All is One." Many Westerners went to study with Ramana at

Arunachala in India from the 1930s until his death in 1950. In Lucknow, India, H.W. L. Poonja, better known as Papaji, was another disciple of Ramana.

I had heard the name Papaji before. But I hadn't paid much attention because I thought the Eastern traditions had nothing to offer me. Years before, I had studied Yogananda's teachings, attended Vipassana meditation retreats, dabbled in Buddhism. None of these pursuits ever gave me a sense of fulfillment, only frustration. There were no states of bliss or even stillness. For a long time, I dismissed any teaching that came from the East, and all the teachers whose names ended in "ji."

But now I was ready to take a fresh look. I learned that Papaji influenced countless seekers, including Gangaji who was one of Papaji's first students to return to the West and give *satsang*. While it was interesting to get familiar with the different players on this stage, it was of greater value to discover what they all had in common, the fundamental premise of the *direct path*: *you are that which you seek*. This is the same message that Eckhart Tolle shares—but with a Western style. I soon discovered that there were many ways of saying the same, simple truth.

I decided to deepen my understanding of this new path and attend Pamela's week-long retreat in northern New Mexico. My friend Ulli joined me. Since the day we met nearly 20 years ago, Ulli and I have shared the same longing, a kind of passion for the "path." I could always count on her to read a book I was excited about or attend a workshop with me. It was no surprise that Ulli made plans to join me without any hesitation when I told her she had to meet Pamela. I drove north from Santa Fe, Ulli drove south from Telluride, and we met just in time to set up our camp and make it to the morning *satsang*.

After the silence at the beginning, I opened my eyes, and Pamela was gazing right back. I melted, and tears spontaneously arose.

There was this knowing without a doubt that I am the same loving presence I saw in Pamela's eyes, a mirror reflecting back my true nature. What I have been looking for all these years is right here inside of me. It was both a relief and a joke. I laughed and cried at the same time.

What made this moment so profound was the realization that Pamela is like me. She's about the same age, has a similar background, loves chocolate, and likes to hike. Pamela has a normal name. And she's a woman. It wasn't a big leap to realize that if Pamela can know her true nature, why not me? Always before, it felt like this realization was out of reach, something for another lifetime, or for someone else more spiritual or evolved. But now here was an ordinary woman just like me that was awakened. As my mirror, she was reflecting back the very essence of my being. Call it consciousness, presence, awareness, the mystery, life, stillness. It doesn't matter. These are just words describing the indescribable truth of who we are.

So if this is who we are, it is obvious that there is no need to search for anything. That's what the *direct path* is all about. In fact, the very act of seeking keeps us from resting, and it is only when we are at rest that our true nature reveals itself. It's nothing fancy. It isn't what I imagined awakening or enlightenment to be. That was part of my problem. Once I imagined enlightenment was desirable, I thought it was something to have, something to possess, a goal to obtain. But that's impossible because there is no "me" to get enlightened. Quite the opposite, the separate "me" disappears when awakening occurs.

After I met Pamela, I wondered if there were others like her. I found that indeed, there are! I was particularly interested in women because it became apparent that there was something unique about the feminine approach.

In general, men tend to talk about the Absolute, the transcendent, the formless. Realizing one's true nature as formlessness is the first step, the approach most of us are familiar with when we think of the old paradigm of enlightenment. But there's another half of the same coin: the world of form including relationships, emotions, love, and compassion. Bringing that into the world—living life fully—is the completion of the circle, sometimes called embodiment.

I see it as the union of the Divine and the human, or the masculine and feminine, or the union of wisdom and love. Embodiment is the juicy, messy side of life. If we leave out our humanness, spirituality can become dry, intellectual, and boring. While there are now male teachers who offer this same perspective, it is women who seem to more fully embrace and integrate the nitty-gritty of daily life.

The women I spoke with live regular lives—with kids, husbands, dogs, meals to cook, and bills to pay. Yes, they literally radiate peace and presence, but they also experience the inevitable challenges of life—divorce, death, cancer, conflict. Though I call them "teachers" for lack of a better word, that's not a term the women themselves use because it implies they know something we don't. They take away the illusion of separation and call themselves "friends."

In my conversations and research, I found that there are three "tributaries" that influenced most of the women I interviewed:

Advaita—the ancient Hindu philosophy of non-duality as expressed through Papapji and Ramana;

Adyashanti—a well-known teacher and author from the Bay Area whose background is in the Zen Buddhist tradition;

The Power of Now—a best-selling book by Eckhart Tolle that facilitates the practice of being fully present in each moment.

Each tributary has its own flavor and sometimes different vocabulary, but each says essentially the same thing: the love, the wisdom, the peace you are looking for is always available, right here, right now. It's not found in a teacher or in a book, not even in the magic of the starry sky.

As you read the stories of these remarkable yet ordinary women, it is my sincere hope that they will be a mirror for you. And in their reflection, you will see the extraordinary truth of who you really are.

The following interviews were conducted from the fall of 2002 to the spring of 2004 and are presented in chronological order.

Pamela Wilson

Pamela was born in San Francisco in 1954. She taught the Sedona Method for six years and then discovered Advaita with Robert Adams. Pamela had her recognition with Neelam in 1997 and started offering *satsang* shortly afterwards. She currently lives in Santa Fe with her dog, Honey, when she isn't on the road giving *satsang* in Europe, Central America, Canada and the USA.

CHAPTER 1

PAMELA WILSON

I have these warm, fuzzy welcoming tendencies.
Each expression of being—sorrow or joy, regret or remorse—
everything just wants to come sit with us.
Who we are is the heart of hearts.

It was the first day of the retreat when Ulli boldly asked Pamela if we could get to know her better. I am much more reserved about that kind of thing, but Pamela wasn't the least bit bothered. Instead, she invited us to soak with her that afternoon in the hot springs, and she answered question after question about her personal life. That was my first experience of being with a teacher who was more like a friend.

Ulli and I asked Pamela if she would come to Telluride in the fall. She didn't ask for much—a place to stay, good food, and a reasonable number of folks to help pay expenses. The house I owned there hadn't yet sold, and I offered it for the day-long *satsang*. It was big enough to accommodate 30 people in the living room/kitchen area. Ulli handled the marketing and other logistics.

Pamela's ordinariness was never more obvious than when she stayed at my house. It was like having a roommate. I was relaxed, and so was Chris. That's saying a lot. "Chris isn't into all this stuff," I told Pamela while we were preparing dinner. I warned her that it would be the first spiritual event he had attended. "What a wise soul," she responded, "waiting for the final teachings." We laughed.

During her stay, I watched how Pamela related to Chris. There was no judgment, no expectations, just genuine respect flowing naturally. She asked him questions about his experience teaching difficult kids. She cared about his answers. Once she made a comment to me, "He's got that twinkle in his eyes."

During *satsang*, someone asked how to deal with her teenage daughter who was caught lying. Pamela offered an image of the mother bowing down to the daughter, literally placing her head under the feet of the child. She suggested that the child, or anyone else, will intuitively know if you feel respect for them or not. "And if you don't, they will resist you," she said to the mother. Pamela explained she had always had difficulty with her father until she did the same thing, inwardly bowing down to him. Though she never told him what she was doing, the relationship between them changed after that. There was less tension, more ease.

I imagined Chris probably felt the same lack of respect Pamela's father once felt. I decided to try an experiment during that weekend. Inwardly, I placed my head under his feet. I didn't have to *try* to feel respect for him. It arose naturally as I was able to really see him. Yep. There was a twinkle in his eyes. The more I looked for that twinkle, the more it was there.

A month after Pamela came to Telluride, we did the interview at Pamela's little one-bedroom adobe just outside of Santa Fe. It was October and a wild weather kind of day. The clouds were heavy and low, practically scraping the ground, dumping a lot of rain, a delight in the high and dry desert country. There were huge claps of thunder every now and then, followed by the sound of rain pounding earnestly on the roof.

I brought along my dog, Kiva. I knew he would be welcome because Pamela welcomes everything including, maybe even especially, dogs. Her golden retriever, Honey, is almost always at her side. Pamela made tea as I set up the equipment. We sat in comfortable chairs with the recorder between us, the dogs asleep on the floor.

ഇന്ദ്ര

Did you have any childhood experiences you think were unusual or unique in any way?

I remember feeling very shy when I was little and feeling more comfortable with animals and nature than with people. I also remember being very small and looking at the adults when they would get agitated and wondering what the problem was, why they were worried. Then growing up, I found out why they were all so worried. They thought they had to run life and carry it and defend it.

What significant spiritual experiences did you have along the way?

I was living in San Francisco in my youth, and somebody gave me some LSD. I'd never had a drink before or anything. But being an intellectual and scientifically curious, I decided to try it. It was very odd because everything started to reveal its formlessness. The wall started moving, everything started moving, and I went, "Uh-oh... things aren't what they appear to be." [She laughs.] It was a little frightening because it activated all the defenses. I felt everything start to expand and dissolve including the sense of me. There was a very strong intention to hold onto something because there was this idea that everything would just dissolve, and I would never be the same.

And after high school?

I went to Pomona College, and still that same sense of not-belonging was always there. I was plagued by that sense of separation except when I was quiet or in nature.

Then in my final year of college my mother got cancer. That was a real wake-up call. I started to study nutrition right before that, and there was an intense hope it could cure anything. She passed away that summer very quickly which left me with a sense that I had better tend to this inner nervousness and stress. I come from a long line of nervous women—very dear, beautiful women—my grandmother and my mother. My mother was amazingly active and a fabulous mother, but she could really get stressed. I thought, "Well, I'll be the next." So I explored meditation and yoga which was really motivated by the fear of death.

It sounds like the death of your mother was a turning point for you.

Absolutely. When my mother died, I was 21, and it was devastating. I went into shock for about ten years. I was barely functional. My sister took care of me. On the surface it would look like I was pretty normal, but I was in shock.

You've talked about a period of real depression. Was that then?

No, that was later. The life fell apart in the early 1990s where through naïveté, I lost all my money. I had given it all away. I lost my job, and my friends got scared and abandoned me. I don't blame them. It was pretty scary. When people know you as very joyful, having your act together, kind of like a golden girl, and then all of a sudden there's this tragic, falling apart into deep sorrow and depression and feeling suicidal—they head for the hills. They wonder, "What happened to our friend? She's gone. Whoever this one is, we don't like her."

That was gorgeous because there had been spiritual pride, and I think this was the balancing. None of the spiritual tricks worked. I was in such deep sorrow then that I just kept going to *satsang*. And living in northern California, you can go to a lot of *satsang*. I would get myself there and just sit. I didn't have a need to listen to every word. It was just like taking refuge in something simple, something quiet, something that was very welcoming.

It does seem like the awakening experience or recognition is often preceded by a loss or a kind of depression.

Well, it used to be that way regularly, but that's not the case anymore. Maybe it was just the "hard nuts."

I remember you saying that you went down many paths...

I started with TM. That was great because during my meditation, I could feel this peacefulness, but then I would go into ordinary life and get stressed and reactive and frustrated. I tried actualization, Insight, EST. Next, I found the Sedona Method which was really helpful because it was like a walking meditation that would return the body-mind or "me" back to a state of peace, but it didn't sever the knot of identification.

You have talked about how the Sedona Method is a focus on releasing the emotions, and now you seem to welcome those feelings instead.

Right. Because when I used to release, there was an opposition or an agenda behind the releasing... "I am going to get rid of this because I don't like this feeling." Now we are noticing that everything is consciousness. Consciousness is emotions, and thoughts, and sensations, and the body, and the mind, and all the people at work. If there is resistance to anything— feelings, thoughts, people—they feel it, your emotions feel it, and it just adds to the agitation. It doesn't soothe it. Opposition is impractical. It doesn't work.

Your quest led you down all these different paths. Were any of them satis-fying?

What I didn't really understand is that I was thinking I was my role, "I am Pamela." That is what was creating all the trouble. I kept trying to fix the personality. There was awareness that the personality was not loving enough, not clear enough, so I was trying to find ease for the personality, to be natural and undefended.

Now I realize that a personality, by nature, can have percentages of that naturalness, be fairly unveiled, but if you think you're "someone," it will just recreate everything. That was humbling, all that work. [She laughs].

Because you'd fix it like a sweater where you darn it in one area, and it starts to unravel in another, and then you go over and crochet it back together, and then it starts unraveling in another area. *DARN IT!* [We laugh.] Must be something wrong with my darning...

For those of us who haven't had this so-called awakening yet, what makes you different from us?

I don't have any doubt about who I am. But if you look inside, you don't have any doubt either. Thought has doubt. Your true nature is openness, not the thinking mind. The mind is basically a doubting, defensive function, right? It has a practical function—to make distinctions, to oppose, to defend, to doubt. But behind its role, it's the same consciousness.

It seems like you are less identified with the separate self.

No, don't go there because you see that's a big extrapolation from, "I just don't have doubt." Everybody can claim their body-mind gets identified and not identified. The only real difference between someone who has remaining doubt and someone who doesn't have remaining doubt is that we don't believe sensations and thoughts and emotions refer to us, to who we truly are. Thoughts and emotions refer to the body-mind.

How did that happen for you, realizing that doubt was just thinking mind and nothing more?

Just grace, really, sitting in *satsang*. Before that, I had amazing spiritual experiences, but I didn't have someone to make it clear, to say, "Do you notice that the so-called spiritual experience was pointing to this... that you are formless intelligence, that you are not contained by the body?"

There was a strong intention, a very strong intention [to awaken] because anything else was way too uncomfortable. Being human can be unbearable because you are "fathomless being" wearing a sensitive instrument. Now as "fathomless being" we can feel endlessly, we can feel with so much depth. To be human on top of that, to know you can die, it raises the stakes. Ordinary life has that flavor of survival all through it. I was just looking for this ability to be at rest, to be like my dog, really. [She chuckles.] I just wanted to feel safe wherever I went, to feel safe with whomever I was with.

If you had a metaphor to describe your recognition, what would you say?

It was very soft. It was like rivers coming together and merging. It was very, very soft. I was just sitting in *satsang* with Neelam. There was this love, this drawing itself into itself.

The interesting thing is after recognition, Neelam went to Europe, leaving this freshly-hatched innocent nothingness. It was great because it turned me within for counsel. There would be this wondering, this curiosity, and the answer would just arise up from silence. The gift from that is now I invite others to ask inside rather than get all the answers from outside. It strengthens the recognition that natural intelligence is always here, the Source of everything in everybody.

One of the things I am interested in is how you embody this perspective in everyday life. If I were a spider on the wall watching as your day unfolds, would it look any different?

No.

Would you yell at someone on the telephone?

I wouldn't yell at someone on the telephone, but yesterday I was driving around, and I did have some words for somebody. But not yelling. I don't have the energy to get really reactive anymore, so my ability to be truly

Shakespearian has been edited. But it's still clean the house, make the food. It's exactly the same as life before, but worry has been reduced by 90 per cent, sense of separation has been reduced by 98 per cent. There's a total knowing. I can't even call it trust because it is so much stronger than that. Life is totally taking care of everything. Who I am, who everyone is—is life. We can all relax, and let life do all the work.

That's one of my favorite quotes from you: "Why not let life do the work? Why not trust the force that grows the beard?"

Yeah, why not. I was recently trying to get a new car, and there was this effort to figure out which car would be the most practical and get the best gas mileage. My mind was saying, I should get a hybrid, but I don't want to get a hybrid. I should get a four-wheel drive, but I don't want to get a four-wheel drive. Finally, there was frustration because that sort of mind activity hasn't happened very often in the last few years. It's funny that it got activated by this whole car thing. So I finally said out loud, "Just decide what car you're going to get, and go get it." And instantly the next day—it was done.

What did you get?

I got a turbo diesel VW Golf that gets 46 mpg. Life did it—life kept going to the VW dealer. Vast intelligence is behind thinking thought. This vast intelligence is not subject to the opposites. For some reason, I went into the old habit of trying to figure out which car to get through thought which always does the pros and cons, the opposites... it was a disaster and very humbling. So old-fashioned!

Let's talk about relationships. You were married in the past, I know.

I was married to a beautiful Italian gentleman who was very kind and brilliant. In my naïveté, I listened to a teacher at the time who said that if all your spiritual work is about maintaining harmony in the relationship, then you shouldn't be married. He said you should use all your spiritual inquiry and work for freedom. So I told my husband that I didn't want to be married anymore. It was a lack of discernment on my part and also, I would suggest, a lack of discernment on the teacher's part.

Partnership can be *satsang*. It can be living and embodying the truth which is the great promise of humanness... embodying kindness, clarity, forgiveness. It's about being best friends, really. That's what relationship is.

Relationship gets projected on by thought. It projects its dissatisfaction onto the relationship. You could be with an embodiment of intelligence, and strength, and courage, and kindness, and your mind would say, "Well, that's very nice BUT they don't do this... "

Wash the dishes.

Yeah. Here's this beautiful being, and thought has to scrape up an argument about what's imperfect about this person because heaven forbid they could just be who they are. Oh gosh. It's thought trying to create separation out of nothing, trying to create separation about how they squeeze the toothpaste tube, or they don't fold their socks correctly.

Or worse yet, they're not spiritual enough.

Meanwhile if you look in their eyes, there's this twinkling, kind, welcoming presence. And thought is going, "They don't read the books and go to the meetings." And they're going, "Hello, I'm just naturalness... wouldn't that be enough? Wouldn't that be enough?"

Is there a time when a relationship may not serve you? And how will you know?

Your body will tell you. I like listening to the body more than thought because thought has a definite agenda. The body is innocent, it's just natural intelligence. You want to first soften the defenses in the body to get to the clarity behind it because sometimes the defenses in the body might say "no" whereas that gentleness right behind it might be saying, "Yes, this is right."

If you go back to resting as best friends, the whole body is soothed. If you think they're your husband or boyfriend, you will have concepts about how husbands and boyfriends should be just as they will project and have concepts about how girlfriends and wives should be.

At the heart of the union is beingness devoted to "itself." That's all life is: beingness using itself to liberate itself, to adore itself, to support itself, to nourish itself, to enjoy itself and to express its vast love. It just wants to touch and taste and smell and dance.

Can you talk about your relationship to money and how you plan or not for the future?

All I do is respond from moment to moment. What we all notice if we look, if we don't listen to thought's interpretation, is that we are being breathed and animated by life. And if you look back on your life, you'll see that you've always been taken care of. There have been very scary moments, but we've survived it. And I don't see that it's Pamela's life anymore, it's just life. And life is very, very wise. It is a lot wiser than any individual could be.

I like looking into the function at the heart of everything. So the function of money—which no one has any problem with—is shelter, food, warmth in the winter, sharing with your friends, being able to pay the bills. So, when I think of money, I see that money isn't money. It's shelter, it's food, it's heartfelt "givingness."

When people donate for *satsang*, they're not giving me money. They're giving me shelter, food and warmth, a new car, warm sweaters. If that's not love, I don't know what love is. It's like a trade... you give me food and a warm sweater, and I will show you how to find the peace within. So it's this gorgeous exchange.

Tell me a little bit about your relationship with your dog, Honey.

My apparent pet... my best friend. It is so clear that dogs are not dogs, cats are not cats, horses aren't horses. It's *being* hanging out with itself, what a rare opportunity with a pet. We call them pets, but they're best friends, and they don't project as often as your human best friend. They have wonderfully low standards. [She chuckles.] They are content with love, shelter, warmth, food, walks. You can't really call them relationships because there's not two. It's just fuzzy beingness and relatively hairless being hanging out.

How did you start offering satsang?

I had gotten fired from the Sedona Institute because I kept putting *satsang* flyers in the back of my classes. The guy who was the head of it asked me not do that because it was threatening him financially. I didn't know what to do because at the time, I had given all my money away. I would tell my friends, "OK, I can be a cook or I can work in a ladies dress shop," and they said, "No, you're going to give *satsang*." I said, "No I am not. What would I say? All is well... rest, rest."

Then, out of the blue, someone from Seattle invited me to come talk to their meditation group, and that's how it started. There was this seeing that life gives *satsang*. This apparent mind-body doesn't give *satsang*, life does it. Life does everything. That was a great relief.

Why Pamela Wilson instead of another name?

I was given lots of beautiful Hindu names, and because I had three different ones, I thought I would ask Mira who was Papaji's beloved, now named Ganga, to decide. I said, "OK, all these beautiful names, and I don't know which one to use. Since you're the elder of this lineage, can you just decide?" And she said, "Do you know what giving a name points to?" And I said, "Yes, it's love giving itself a name that points to its true nature." Ganga went through all the names, she would say them out loud, look at me, and she would say the next one out loud and look at me. All of a sudden she said in her Belgian accent, "What about Pamela?" I went, "OK—so be it."

So, the name was returned which I like because it's ordinary. It's further confirming that we're all the same. These so-called *satsang*-givers are no different than the person they're speaking to. It's just life speaking to itself. And that's what's happening now.

What is happening now?

Being appears to be waking up everywhere, and *being* isn't as interested in hierarchy and distinctions the way it used to be. The interest now is in sameness. What is the same in all the traditions? What is the same in the Absolute and the relative? What is the same in human beings? To me, that is very intriguing. It's like the content and all the distinctions were just veils, attributes and appearances. Now everyone is going... hmm, I wonder what is at the heart of the matter.

It does seem like this awakening phenomenon is happening more frequently. And when someone like you shares your story, it makes it clear that you are no different than "us."

Everyone is this naturalness. When we start calling it enlightenment and awakening, thought can use that to compare, right? But if we say this naturalness or this simple presence—thought can't run a comparison study. The whole invitation is to look prior to language, prior to concepts, prior to thought's projection.

What's looking and what's seeing? There's not that much there. There's just this simple, ordinary presence, and it is so unadorned. You can run right by it if you're looking for something fancy. It's always been here, it has no age, it doesn't really have any properties or qualities, it's just this intelligence. It's so quiet, that's why they call it silence. [She laughs.]

One last thing. How do you see the role of women right now? I know it is all the same message, and yet there may be something different about the way women deliver it.

Well, first of all, there's only *being*, so there really are no men or women. I have to start there with the absolute truth. Then as *being* embodies in a feminine expression and a masculine expression, there is uniqueness to those embodiments—and thank God! I am all for sameness, but the expression of uniqueness is so delicious, and I don't think anyone would like that to subside.

What I notice in this feminine expression here is that I don't see a difference between the Absolute and the relative. I don't see a difference between emptiness and form. After recognition, there was just this quiet openness, this "yes." One day fear showed up, and I heard thought say, "Fear? What is fear doing here?" Then I heard wisdom say, "Fear is welcome here." I went, "Oh I see, everything is welcome, *everything*." I have these warm, fuzzy welcoming tendencies. Each expression of being— sorrow or joy, regret or remorse—everything just wants to come sit with us. Who we are is the heart of hearts.

It may be that I am just projecting on all these emotions, but they all seem to want to come home. So I invite everyone to be that way inside, to be this kindness that we are. There is no one required to be kind because *who we are* is kindness.

So is there anything unique about the feminine expression of beingness?

In the realm of appearances, it can appear that the male embodiments are pointing more towards the Absolute. Again, it is just the play of appearance. So you go to the guys, and they're saying, "Absolute, Absolute, Absolute," and the women are saying, "Tenderness, kindness, just permeate it with love." *Being* is this fierce clarity that demands only the Absolute, and *being* is also this soft invitation to welcome everything and bring it into the heart.

₮₧₲

At that moment, a neighbor's dog came wandering into the yard, our dogs started barking, and that was the end of the interview. We took a walk with the dogs in the arroyo near Pamela's house, huddling together under the umbrella when a shower passed by. It was like seeing Kiva for the first time… fuzzy beingness, my best friend. Pamela told me several months later that she is writing a book from Honey's perspective, something about a golden retriever's guide to enlightenment.

I drove home to my little house in Santa Fe, thinking about what Pamela shared about relationships. Though what she said applies to all relationships, it certainly seemed specific to me and the expectations I had placed on Chris. I remembered what she said about the body knowing when it is time to leave. Chris was like an anchor for me, a solid presence whenever I leaned up against him or curled up in his arms. Yes, the body has its own wisdom. I began to listen to what it was telling me.

Sharon Landrith

Sharon was born in 1947 in a little town in Kansas. She was asked by Adyashanti to give *satsang* in 2003. Sharon lives in Crestone, Colorado with her husband and practices as a medical intuitive. She has two children and two grandchildren.

CHAPTER 2

SHARON LANDRITH

Often there's still a thread that says
the "me" is going to get it,
the "me" is going to wake up.
And it just isn't true.
It actually wakes up out *of the "me."*

A round the same time I met Pamela, I learned about Adyashanti from a friend who kept a dog-eared and underlined copy of Adyashanti's book next to her bed. She described Adyashanti as a clear teacher, someone whose presence was big enough to feel when in the same room. I didn't want to miss him when he came to Santa Fe.

It's always interesting when you first see a person that you have heard a lot about. Your mind can't help but have certain expectations. So, when Adyashanti walked into the room, I was a little startled by how small, almost fragile he looked. Not bigger than life, the way I imagined. It was no accident that there was a plastic statue of Yoda from Star Wars fame sitting on the altar. There was definitely a kind of resemblance—shaved head, big ears and slight build. He had a kind of other-worldly presence to him, like an alien with a message for the human race.

Adya, as he's affectionately called, is in his 40s. Wearing a cotton short-sleeved shirt tucked into his blue jeans, he got comfortable in the big chair on the stage, looked around the room, and then closed his eyes. After a time of silence, he spoke. I immediately dug in my purse for my notebook, knowing I wanted to try and capture his "pointing-out" instructions. That term refers to the Zen story about how you can't really give someone the experience of the moon, but you can point to it so they can look in that direction and experience it for themselves.

Adya's following is dedicated. I had to stand in line at least an hour in order to get a decent seat. Even then I wasn't near the front, but it was a perfect seat, because I was sitting right next to Sharon Landrith whom I didn't know at the time. Sharon was the first person to get on stage to sit next to Adya when he opened it up to the audience. Her blonde-gray hair was wound up in a soft bun on top of her head; she was dressed elegantly but comfortably. There was a certain presence about her, an ease. I guessed she was in her 50s.

Adya welcomed Sharon warmly, and she thanked him for the opportunity to be sitting with him. I assumed that they knew each other as student/teacher. Sharon didn't say exactly what she was afraid of, but it was about a possible loss if she kept going deeper into truth.

Adya explained to Sharon that in the old days, people on a spiritual path left everything first, let go of all worldly attachments, joined a monastery. "Now," he said, "we are having to do the letting-go later, not first. And whatever your life preserver is, whatever you're hanging onto will be challenged. It's a bumpier ride because you don't solve it by leaving the world. People are being called back into life to fully live it."

Over the weekend, he talked a lot about the process of embodiment, a new learning for me. I had assumed that once you have an experience of bliss, merging with all-that-is, you were done, you had arrived. That's one of the many myths of enlightenment. That merging experience is not even necessary. If it does happen, it turns out that it really is just the beginning.

Adya is known as an embodiment teacher. Many people who see him have already had some kind of an awakening, and they need help in integration. Adya is very much a part of the world, not cloistered away in an ashram. He's married, he loves bicycle racing, he won't be put on a pedestal. He is clear about that, joking about how he eats at McDonald's and plays poker.

The next day at the intensive, I recognized an acquaintance from Colorado. I wandered over to where Marcee was talking to Sharon and was introduced. Marcee explained that Adyashanti has cultivated a garden of blossoming teachers, "Adya's girls," and Sharon was one of them. Sharon planned to be in Colorado in the fall to give *satsang*, only half an hour's drive from my house. Sharon expressed interest in being a part of the book, so I made plans to be in Colorado for her *satsang* in September and to do the interview.

I interviewed Sharon at Marcee's house. It was one of those glorious fall days when summer still lingers in the warm sun, but the snow has already blanketed the high peaks. I set up the equipment in a small meditation room in Marcee's "earthship" house, built into the hillside of a pinyon-juniper forest.

ΩϾ

Let's start with something about your early days, defining moments that you can share with us.

I lived in a very isolated place, the middle of central Kansas, and there was no talk about anything that was unusual. Yet, there was a guiding point in my life. At the time, I thought it was union with God. I'd be walking to school and standing on a corner, and there would be this feeling of being taken in a certain kind of way by this whole lighted being. Here I was, a kid, and yet there wasn't any fear or any question. It would be this timeless, unified golden moment, then it would be over, and I would continue on my walk to school and wouldn't even really think about it.

The point of that is if I can see one consistent theme all the way through, it was that love and desire for what I thought was union with God. That was the leading compass.

You were definitely a seeker.

Always. First it was in the church, which was the Methodist Church. But at 16, I remember walking out of church and saying, "My God isn't your God—the God that says if you're not baptized, you go to hell." Christianity did not fit what I knew inside.

It was Buddhism that first opened the door. When I started to hear the teachings and read the different books, I felt a resonance. I was given all sorts of techniques and went to lots and lots of retreats. Always without exception, the techniques would fall away, and this presence that became deeper and vaster, would happen.

I was never drawn into the dogma of it or the teachings of it. At first, I didn't realize that it was just opening up what was already there. I thought it was in the meditation, it wasn't in me. Eventually it became consistent enough that I began to sense that it has to be somewhere inside because just sitting down and becoming silent, it would pop open. This presence would just be there.

It was when I met Jean Klein 16 years ago that the door really opened. We read about him in *Yoga Journal* while living in Kansas. We heard the truth in this interview, so we packed our bags and flew to California for a ten-day retreat that he held once a year. He abided in and transmitted what he called the flame, the flame of being. He described it in such clear and poetic ways of what had been happening all my life, those visitations, those tastes, but I had no words for them. He gave both the words and the transmission so profoundly, it was awakened, and then it was understood.

He taught a beautiful form of yoga called Kashmir yoga which emphasized the energy body. It was his way of giving tools of transformation, not going through the mind and trying to see patterns and figure them out, but going directly to the body and the energy body. As a doctor, he was really adept in that. It began to soften the boundaries and that cage that we all think we are, into something that's very vast and boundless. That was a beautiful gift.

But, I would look around, and it didn't seem like realization was taking place. I found it strange, here we are with this master who says it's there constantly, it's everywhere, it's who we are, and yet no one seems to be getting it.

It sounds like people including you would get it for a moment or two, a day or two, but then it would be gone.

Yeah, the seeker's curse—got it, lost it, got it, lost it. With Jean Klein, essential shifts took place that never really went away, but the good side effects that we all like would go away.

The side effects would be bliss?

Bliss and calmness and everything is all one. Of course, then there would be the opposite and perfect polarity of that which would be lots of material coming to the surface. My tendency as a person was to have a lot of suffering thoughts. Depression was in my family—mother, sister, brother—everyone had depression. So when it would come up, I thought I was losing it, and then I became grief stricken because I wanted it more than anything   else. I had a full life and was very much in the world, but I really wanted only one thing. So, to feel like I would get it, then lose it, was very difficult. There were times I would try to shut it all out just to save myself that swing, that pain. But of course, that wouldn't last.

Then Jean Klein died. We'd visited Gangaji before, didn't feel particularly drawn to make her the teacher, but we heard what she had to say, and some kind of deep recognition happened. We began to hear about Byron Katie from some people. So the direct way, the Advaita way, started to show up. You'd hear about different people that had seemingly spontaneous awakenings.

It sounds like you were in an in-between place, after Jean Klein, after some serious study with Buddhist teachers and before you met Adyashanti.

We got a flyer in the mail about the Inner Directions conference. There was an article that Adya had written, and it was so beautifully written and so clear. My husband Nate said, "Well, do you want to pack our bags for

California again?" I said "Sure, let's go." [She laughs.]

There were about six hundred people. It was doubling each year from its beginning, because it was so popular. It was just catching on fire. That year, Eckhart Tolle was there and Byron Katie. It was stunning, truly stunning. But we went there because of Adya. We heard what was being spoken, but it was more about recognizing on a very deep level something that was coming through Adya. We came up afterwards, and he very generously held back, gave us some time, responded to one of Nate's questions. We were just profoundly, to the core, touched.

Within three months, we came back to his retreat. At that time, the retreat was still 25 people, so it was a very intimate, very casual setting with him which was precious. We went about four times a year to be with him. It was very accelerated—awakening gets tiring to say—but it was just profound, and it didn't mean that it wasn't also difficult.

What was difficult about it?

Adya had asked me to do *satsang*, and I was such a shy personality, I hadn't even gone up to talk to him in the chair. So, when I gave *satsang*, it blew everything open. It blew silence or awareness open. From that moment on, it did not ever close. But it also opened Pandora's box. There was a pouring out that seemed to be happening, and the force of it just exploded. I knew what was happening, thank God.

But it was out of control. You realize you have stepped out of a plane—you took some sort of step into an abyss, and now you know that you're not stepping back. [She laughs.] You know that the mind has never been there. Maybe 90 per cent to 95 per cent of the people, and this includes your most intimate people, they do not know anything about this.

Was that fearful?

That has never been a big part. I have physical fears, for example of huge waves in the ocean, but not fears of the void. Jean Klein called it the silence, but I didn't know what it was back then. It was just nothing. But nothing, of course, is so vast, so pregnant, and so awesome. I've been a retreat leader when people have touched that void and have just gone off, crying, freaked out and terribly afraid, wanting to leave and all sorts of things. But that was never my experience. In fact, it's home and profound contentment. It was really always the opposite.

Even when you were asked to give satsang*, there was no fear?*

There was self-consciousness, of being shy, that part was fearful. That was a beautiful gift because the love of Adya, and the love of the truth was so in place that it just burned it all up.

Is that self-consciousness gone?

It's gone. There can be certain circumstances, but they're very rare; there'll be a nervousness in your stomach or in your throat, but so what. It's just a little bit of nervousness. It's not a big deal. Something blew out so profoundly when that happened [giving *satsang*], that there was some presence, some vastness that began to speak and began to use this body. There was no doubt that that's what was happening. None. I can get up in front of anybody and ask any question or I can do *satsang* and there's no fear, nothing.

I suppose you grow to trust that.

You do, because you know it's not you. And it is you in that there's no separation. It's not my will but thy will. You also realize that to own it, to feel special about it or to grasp it, that's the very split that's going to obscure it. So the way is to totally surrender to that, and then Source does its thing. It's very interesting, the exact opposite of pride and specialness.

You know you can't own it. There's this deep knowing that it's in the very absence that presence appears. Right now what's going on is that there's this emptying out and just saying yes, yes, yes.

That's a theme I've heard before, saying yes.

There's no other way. I think it must be trust that starts to happen, then there's a deeper realization that trust isn't the issue. It's just yes. It's truth. So it's saying yes to truth, yes to wholeness, yes to joy without cause, yes to reality. I think it was last year where the personal identity was collapsing, and there were painful moments.

How did that look for you?

It really started accelerating with Adya... that swinging from got it/lost it, there was a seeing through of that. The Buddhists call it the middle way. Then the swinging back and forth, the coming, the going, the getting it, the losing it, all happens in the light of awareness. And then there is no coming and going. There's something that's stable and constant, the true essence, the true nature.

Some ways of defining myself—habits, belief structures, neuroses—they just blew away, they no longer function. Others come back, and come back. Sometimes it's painful things that are let go of, that are brought forward and revealed. But there's no judgment which is really a remarkable relief. Judgment just isn't there. The pain is more in the letting go. The mind becomes fearful. For me, it's passed now, but it was over personal relationships and, quote, *my* life.

I remember when you spoke in July in front of the group in Santa Fe, there was some fear. What was that about?

I thought I was going to lose all my friends. I had observed it with people who "woke up," and they stayed at home, and they taught. There was no other life. I liked my life, I had a very rich life, good friends. They weren't especially awake, but they were good, conscious people and lived good lives. I didn't want to step out of that. I think that was the fear. And of course, none of that happened. Some friends have fallen away, and there are some activities that I am no longer drawn to. In a very natural way that has happened, but it was not a sacrifice. I realized it was the personal identity dying. There's some attachment there, and then it passes.

There was a period of time where there were a lot of things arising that had been shoved below the surface like irritation, self-righteousness, "I'm right and you're wrong," with very close friends. That was very distressing, and yet I knew what was happening. There was just this resting, resting, letting it happen. Then like all the other difficult passages that had happened, I woke up one morning, and it was all gone. And in the background was just love. The personal identity and the subtle judgments that I wasn't even aware of were exposed, liberated, and in its place, there was love.

It doesn't sound like there's a lot of doing here.

No doing, that's the joke. It's spontaneous, it just happens. There's a compassion that seems to be available. I think that's why there's no judgment that comes up, not even with deep, deep shadows that have really been locked off... when that's exposed, it's just ahhhhh. It's a classic teaching story in a way, the mother includes all her children, the creator includes all of its creation.

I haven't had the experiences you've had, but there's a part of me that understands this process of embodiment.

There's a resonating, absolutely. "It" resonates when it hears truth, when it hears itself. I think that's the great gift of *satsang*, really. It's the transmission, it stimulates and resonates. It's the same that's being spoken within you, within everyone... it starts to resonate, resonate, resonate and it just wakes up.

If I ask, "Where did the waking up happen?" I realize that *it wakes up out of the "me."* The "me" keeps thinking that if it does this or doesn't do that or if it lets go of this or if it understands that... it's still caught in the karmic wheel of the "me." It actually wakes up *out* of the "me." Then it seems to, in this very mysterious but profoundly intelligent way, come back and claim the body-mind structure.

It's astonishing—95 per cent of the people I talk to in my intuitive work are in that process. Often there's still a thread or a flavor that says the "me" is going to get it, the "me" is going to wake up. And it just isn't true. All the teachers say that, but you don't get it until it really takes place.

I've always had a critical nature. I wanted to get it. I wanted to know it. I wanted the "me" to be perfect. I thought that in waking-up, the "me" would be a perfect, pure vehicle for that. And actually, there's incredibly neurotic flavors moving through this person. It's seen with a sort of affection, sometimes humor, because I don't know whether this human being will ever be perfect. I doubt it [she laughs], but it doesn't matter.

It's almost as if the human condition by definition is not perfect.

Absolutely. That's the joke of it. But you see over and over that wholeness rights itself. There are areas of the life that are conditioned and discordant, and with mysterious wisdom, it just starts to fall away, to re-orchestrate, re-order. But I don't think perfection is possible. The mind-body process is conditioning, that's what it is.

I want to talk about your relationship with Nate. You have really shared this path together.

Yes, and sharing the same teachers in the same way. I think it's been the grace of our relationship. There are three areas where we're bound. It's that connection, first and foremost, it's the love of nature in all forms—hiking, camping, taking trips, and a love of having fun. We love to celebrate life, whether that's with friends, great food.

At the same time, we are really quite the opposite of the poles. He's very linear, very masculine. I'm very intuitive, right-brain. So in one way, we've really helped each other, in that we've balanced each other and opened up ways of seeing that we probably wouldn't have seen if it weren't for our love for each other that opened that up. But it also caused stress and difficulty.

The more awake, the more open to reality—the more you can observe, celebrate or ignore each other's differences—you realize it has nothing to do with you. Before, at least for me, and I think Nate too, I was caught up in this idea that if he didn't respond or react or hear or see or be a way that I wanted him to be, it was a personal thing.

I'm pretty verbal, pretty blunt sometimes. If I have a truth or if I'm seeing something, it just blurts out, that's just how it is. He's quite the opposite, very reticent, won't say much, would rather get his head chopped off than to speak highly-charged emotions. Our relationship went through some real adjustments when the waking-up happened for me. There were certain places that had to be talked about or dealt with, and there were some pretty shaky moments for us.

You had your waking-up experience at one of Adya's retreats. As I recall, it was the coming-home part where it got interesting.

It was the coming home and the rearranging of the relationship and my life. When wholeness starts to move through your life, it's going to bring everything into balance, into truth. And what isn't truth is going to be exposed.

In those years of rearranging, can you give us a specific example of how you had to do that?

For us, it was almost archetypal patterns. One of the things I was saying and I hear many women say is, "He does not see me or hear me." And that was big for us, big. I had brought it out in many different ways, but it was met with a wall. We had perfect patterns. His was with his mother and sister, mine was with my father. We met each other perfectly. So there would be these walls, and nothing moved.

Because I'm the more verbal one, which often happens in male-female relationships, I just brought it out. "Is this how you feel? And is this how you see it? What's going on? This is how I feel." It wasn't said in a mean way. It was, "Let's get it out on the table." The reality of it was very difficult for me to accept. Everything I thought that he was thinking, he actually was. [She laughs.] It was shocking.

Finally I had an interview with Adya. I hardly ever brought personal stuff to him; I just thought that wasn't his job. But this was so big and so up for me. I said, "One of my main things going on is that I've not ever been heard, especially by the males in my life, and there's a lot of resentment around that, a lot of defense." He just laughed and said, "What's new? Every woman I've talked to says the same thing. It's true, isn't it?" "Yes," I said, "it's true."

Adya told me, "Until you can give that to yourself, until you can literally turn back into the core and let awareness pour that through the body-mind structure and really listen, you will always look for it outside, and it will never happen." It was just like that—that's one of the great gifts of a teacher—in that truth, in that profound clarity, realization can take place. And it happened right there.

It just liberated it.

We were in California at the time, and for nine days I could have ripped Nate apart limb by limb. I was furious. It was the rage, I think, of all women through the centuries. And I knew it. I knew to keep my mouth shut. I just stayed with it and stayed with it. It was so huge that there wasn't any escaping it. I knew what was happening. I knew just to be with it. Then it passed. One morning I woke up, and it was gone. And I never, ever asked that of him again. I would tease him sometimes. And if I really wanted to be heard, I was heard. He either liked it or didn't. No more was I looking to him to do that for me. It's like asking for love from everyone, and it cannot happen until there's that pouring the love into oneself.

That's a great teaching for all of us and helpful to share because I think you're right, it's so archetypal.

I'll tell you what; it was a pretty intense nine days. [We laugh.] But finally that realization got through; it's not personal. If there is only One then everything that happens for one person happens for all beings, especially something like that which is so archetypal, so classic in our society. A lot of rage lives within the male and female. They need a place for it to be liberated. If it can be liberated with some sort of awareness, then it lightens it.

What's it like now for the two of you as a result of your recognition when Nate hasn't had the same experience? Does it create separation between you?

It did. How he dealt with it is he just ignored it, acted like it wasn't happening. I resented him for that. Then it moved to where it really made no difference to me at all. In fact, this is a funny little story. It was the last retreat we had gone to when we were in California, and it was at that retreat that Adya asked me to teach. Again, it was totally out of the blue. I was deeply touched and profoundly grateful.

At the end of the group, we were all in this huge circle where people were speaking a few words during the closing, and Nate was way in the back. Adya said he wanted a blessing for Sharon so that when she leaves, she would have a blessing of the sangha [the community]. It was very beautiful. Then it was over. I'm racing around, and several people who lived in Iowa or different areas in the Midwest were getting my name because there's very few people in that area doing this kind of teaching.

We're on our way, and I realize Nate hasn't said a word. He hasn't acknowledged what happened at all. I tuned in, and it was just fine. There was no need for the acknowledgement. It was totally free. We're talking, and I don't even remember how it came up. I said, "I wonder how that's going to work when I go home, about Adya asking me to teach." And he asked, "Adya asked you to teach?!" "Yeah, you were there." He said, "I didn't hear that. I was sitting way in the back, and I couldn't really hear what was going on. I thought Adya was just asking a blessing for us on our journey home. I had no idea!" [She laughs.]

There were two gifts there. One, it was of no matter to me. He either acknowledged it or he didn't. The other was, I thought it was interesting that he didn't hear it. [She laughs.] But he was very kind and has been very supportive ever since. More and more, he's softened around it.

In the last few months, it's come to the point where it's no longer personal. What comes up through him, how he sees things, how he doesn't see things, it's really his business, the same with me. We gave each other that agreement at the very first of the relationship, to let each other be who we are. That's been one of our main intentions throughout our relationship, about 18 years now. Now I would say it's truly letting each other just be who they are in a real unconditional way. Love and affection are naturally present.

You have two grown children and two teenage grandkids. How do they view you? Are you accepted by them?

It's a non-issue. My daughter has gone to *satsang* and will occasionally come to things. My son has very genuinely opened up to the more fundamental Christian way. I can see the living spirit in his life, and it's been very beneficial, very helpful for him, but that tends to close down any conversation. There's a beautiful book out with statements from teachers from Buddhism, Christianity and Hinduism, and they are almost word for word the same. I would bring that up to talk to him, try to meet him, and he finally said, "I'm just not interested in that." That's cool, that's OK. So, they really have no idea.

My grandkids think that I am a different kind of grandmother. I heard my granddaughter say something when a friend asked if her grandmother was cool like her mother. She said, "Oh yeah, she's way cool." [She laughs.] They can have conversations with me. My grandson is extraordinarily intuitive. He's kind of closed that down going through puberty, but he could always talk to me about that, and we could discuss things. As far as my being a teacher, my doing anything I do, it's just not a part of their lives. Sometimes I think it would be nice to really share that part. But if you open it, and it's not there, it's not there. Again, it's none of my business.

Describe what you see the role of women is right now.

Something moves through here that has always had this profound connection with the Divine Mother. Linda Johnson wrote a book about six or seven women from India who were fully awake, in most cases they were born awake. In the United States, movie stars are young girls, models, and in India, they're awakened saints. I was so touched by her book that I have made it a point to receive darshan [a transmission] from every one. It's not the goddess, it's the Divine Mother and her many faces.

If there's a uniqueness, the woman teacher seems to include the sacred body, the substance, the everything. In most men teachers, and that's not so with Adyashanti, they emphasize a little more of the transcendence, the emptiness, the non-personal. And here [referring to herself], there's perhaps a little more emphasis on how it functions in the life, in the body, in children, in the world.

But if there is an emphasis, that's it... how does it work as you're doing dishes, as you're being with a friend, as you're driving, as you're cleaning your house, whatever? It's present, the mystery, the revealing, the liberation, the love—all of that is totally present in the most ordinary events. It's awake in that ordinariness… taking a walk, looking at the birds, talking to your grandson.

Is there a quality that you could name as feminine that comes through both the male and female teachers now that hasn't been so present in the teachings before.

Yes. You and I both have been seekers for a long, long time, and how many women teachers have you found until now? There's Gangaji—that was the first thing I said to her, "You're the first woman I have been with that is awake." I was with some wise teachers that certainly knew how to move back and forth between the seen and the unseen, but I had never been with one who was awake other than the Indian women. But, they were totally separate from the world.

Is there any reflection you might have on the ageing process?

I have never minded getting older. In fact, I've always been happier as I've gotten older. I could look and say, "Gosh, I wish my chin wasn't falling," and all of that. Mostly, I've always really enjoyed ageing. It's just a natural process that there's really not very much attachment or engagement about. Occasionally, there will be old conditioning that will come up, but then it just rises and falls away. There's a kind of affection and appreciation for it, an enjoyment of the calmer, quieter, more peaceful place. I don't really pay too much attention to it actually.

Which leads me to the final question… how do you view death?

In truth, if there's birth, there's death. It's a natural fact. When I had a lot more suffering thoughts, I kind of longed for death as a great release and a way to get out, I think, though I never had any suicidal thoughts. I always knew that was not a way. Now there's this sweet affection and such an aliveness in life that has never been experienced. If there was a personal preference, it would be nice to live life this way for a while. [She laughs.] I'm not dismissing life in such a cavalier way as I did before.

If it happens, it happens. Like a tree falls, and it's time for that tree to go. It has nothing to do with the life in that tree or the life that surrounds that tree. There's no misunderstanding that life ends when this body does. There's just a sense that it's happened many times before, it happens every-where, it's constant. It's the in-breath, it's the out-breath, so there really isn't a yearning for it or fear of it. Death naturally happens.

ဆာ

On the drive home to the mesa, I noticed that the golden aspen leaves were beginning to fall; a reminder that winter was around the corner. The same cycle of death that Sharon talked about.

With winter coming, I had to make some decisions. My house hadn't yet sold and there was no way I could stay in Santa Fe if I didn't sell the house. Maybe it was time to move back to Colorado. But I argued with myself, "I'm giving up too easily. I should dig my heels in and try harder to make a 'go' of it in Santa Fe." I didn't want to feel like the move was all a waste, or worse yet—the wrong decision.

The mind was working hard, wound up in the pros-and-cons game that Pamela had described when she was trying to figure out which car to buy. I knew I had to let go of the thinking. My mind was "over its head." It couldn't help me figure it out.

When I got home, I went to visit the twin trees behind the house where my former husband's ashes had been placed some ten years before. On the day of our wedding, Brian and I had walked through these two pine trees on a path to the meadow where we were married. Now there was a bronze plaque there that I had made with this poem engraved on it:

Meet me here in this gateway
Between heaven and earth
Birth and death
Where all things begin and end
And begin again.

I lay on the fragrant earth looking up through the pine needles at the blue, blue sky. The wind chimes played their gentle music. I relaxed, opening to the unknown, to whatever wanted to happen. I remembered what Pamela said, "Why not let life do the work?"

I can't really explain how the "answer" became obvious. Maybe it was the body's wisdom arising, feeling so at home lying on the land I loved. Without really thinking, the idea arose to try and sell the other half of my land. That would get me out of debt but still allow me to keep the house. Leave Santa Fe, return to the mesa, return to Chris. Return home.

I walked into the house, got on the phone to my nearest neighbor to tell them that I was planning on selling the 35 acres between us. I explained that I wanted them to know before I actually put it on the market because it would have a big impact on them if someone else built a house there. They came over in 15 minutes. We walked the land, and they wanted to buy it. Really, it was just like that.

After they left, I was hanging the laundry out on the clothesline feeling amazed about what just happened when a hawk flew overhead. Brian and I had named the land, Flying Hawks, because of its location on a ridge top where the red-tailed hawks liked to soar. When it landed in one of the twin trees, I couldn't ignore the "sign." I paused to watch it. Then I realized it was the day of our anniversary. I smiled.

This was beyond "creating my own reality." I hadn't *done* anything. I couldn't have even imagined this reality. Is this what it's like when you let life do the work? It seemed so easy. More like floating down the river instead of swimming upstream.

Chameli Gad Ardagh

Chameli was born in 1971 in Norway. She came to America in 2001 and has since been co-teaching "The Deeper Love" seminars with her husband, Arjuna. She is the founder of "The Temple Group Network," an international network of women's groups, and is passionately involved in the exploration of a more feminine-influenced spirituality. She is the author of *Come Closer—Spiritual Awakening for the Feminine Heart*, and co-author of *The Temple Group Manual—Guidelines and Feminine Spiritual Practices.*

CHAPTER 3

CHAMELI GAD ARDAGH

So much of my life was about getting love,
there was so much longing for love.
Then to realize that that's what I'm made of,
that love is right here. Wow. It was a very simple realization and an
experience of this big love.

Sometime after talking with Sharon in September, I learned that "Adya's girls" were hosting a *satsang* intensive in the Bay Area—for women, by women. As far as I know, for the first time, there were several teachers sharing the role of *satsang*-giver on a rotating basis. I knew it was a great opportunity to meet these women and hopefully do several interviews.

In late October, I was on the road in my truck camper heading to California. This was a dream from years ago, when I did one of those visualization exercises: describe in detail the activity that would bring you the greatest joy—assume no limitations. I wrote about wanting to travel around the West in a camper interviewing women. I wasn't clear about the topic, but I knew I wanted to travel to beautiful places, and I wanted to talk to women. Since that time, I thought of all kinds of subjects that I might focus on—gardening, ranching, and relationships. Nothing was right until now.

I took the "Loneliest Highway," Highway 50, the most direct route between Colorado and northern California. It's a perfect road for someone who thrives on open spaces, big views, and endless places to camp. I have to admit, though, when I left the town of Ely in a snowstorm and frigid temperatures, I felt a little vulnerable. Cell phones don't work on this stretch of highway, and there's a lot of distance from one little town to the next. It's not a place you want to have car trouble, especially in early winter. My dog, Kiva, is a great companion at times like these, and I was happy for the company.

My anxiety subsided as I drove west. The snow hadn't yet started sticking on the road, so I could relax into the vastness of the rolling terrain. I drove until sunset then started looking for the right road that would take me off the main highway, not too far, but far enough for solitude. I turned off into an abandoned mining area where I settled in for the long, cold night. The clouds parted to reveal a full moon, the snowy landscape white and bright. When I went outside after dinner to pee, I wondered why the moon looked so lopsided. Then I remembered that there was an eclipse that night. I watched for awhile, but it was much too cold to linger. I climbed back into the camper, tucked the extra sleeping bag around Kiva, and burrowed into my own down comforter.

The next day I arrived in Nevada City where a good friend lives and where Chameli and her husband, Arjuna, have their home. I had read one of Arjuna's books and had heard about him from others in the *satsang* community. When I got online to check them out, I was intrigued about the workshops they were offering called "Deeper Love." Their flyer said, "Relating can be the expression of your deepest wisdom and vision."

There was a time that looking for a soul mate was the center of my search, thinking that if I only had the right relationship, the longing would be met, and I would be at peace. It's in relationship that the "rubber meets the road," so I am always curious to explore that topic in my interviews. I emailed Chameli and told her about my book, and she responded with an invitation to interview her after they finished their workshop in Europe.

My friend in Nevada City helped me with the directions to Chameli's house. After driving part way, I stopped to check the directions and realized I had left them behind. I tried calling my friend, but she wasn't home. I couldn't call Chameli because her phone number was also on those directions. "Not to worry," I reminded myself. There was this certainty that somehow I would get there. I kept driving, looking for landmarks I remembered from reading the directions beforehand. My internal compass said I was close, but I couldn't remember the specific number on the house. I stopped randomly and asked a guy who was outside doing yard work if he knew a couple who do workshops. "Is he a writer?" he asked. "Yes," I said. "Kind of quiet?" "Probably," I shrugged, not really knowing if he was quiet or not. "They live across the street."

It was a lived-in, modest house in an ordinary kind of neighborhood. I walked around to the back where I saw muddy boots sitting on the porch. I remembered that Arjuna had two boys from a previous marriage. It was Halloween, and Chameli told me the kids would be gone that day. I knocked a little tentatively; still not sure it was really the right house.

Chameli greeted me with a soft hug. She looked young in the photos, but it wasn't until I met her that I realized how young. Another enlightenment myth busted: age has nothing to do with wisdom. She was dressed in a black top and snug slacks that showed off her curves. There was a warm, cozy fire going. On the glass coffee table, candles were lit and four ripe apples rested on a bright blue plate, like a still life painting. She offered me ginger tea in a small handmade mug, and we settled onto the comfortable couch. While I set up the tape recorder, I asked her to pronounce her name for me. Chameli, like Emily, she said, with a "ch" as in charming, I thought.

ॐ

Let's talk first about your own journey. What got you started?

When I was a child, I was very much pulled to the mystery. I lived in Norway which is very secular, but my neighbor was a Catholic, and I remember begging to come to church with her. I started being passionate about theater and creativity very early in life. For me, theater was the pathway to explore reality outside the mind. It was an intense process I went through. All my teenage years, it was kind of dark. I was experimenting with drugs, searching, experiencing the world in the most total way I knew. Then in my early 20s, I went to north India where the Tibetans lived in exile. The meeting with Tibetan Buddhism was an awakening experience. It was a feeling of coming home. I saw that all I had searched for outside was inside.

I went to India, then back and did theater, back to India, then back to do theater, and back to India again. I was involved with Osho [Bhagwan Shree Rajneesh] for maybe five years. It was not only him but all those years of following a masculine path, with the focus of reaching a goal which colored all my spiritual experiences. I had a very strong idea of what enlightenment should be like, of how it should be something more. Though that idea was created by a masculine psyche, I took that as a reflection of truth. So that's why I went on the hamster wheel of seeking. I did everything... therapy, yoga, meditation, extreme Vipassana, extreme Osho meditation; everything was extreme in exploring these things.

It sounds like you were driven, the call was very strong for you.

Yes, and in the core of that call is a longing that is very innocent, that has no concept of enlightenment or anything. It simply wants to find a way to love fully, to live in a natural, sane way. It is so easy to forget that simple wisdom of the heart when we start to follow spiritual teachers or teachings.

Somehow you got off the hamster wheel.

That happened when I met my teacher, ShantiMayi. She's an American woman, but she lives in a traditional Hindu community in north India, she's part of a lineage there. The work of the ashram is about prayer, how we can bring balance to the world, how we can cultivate love. It was a big contrast to the path that I had been following, which was about *my* freedom, *my* liberation, how can I fix all this stuff in me... it was very focused on *me*. So that's what kicked me out of it. It was awakening to the big picture, the big love—realizing this has nothing to do with me. That was the "ah-ha." That is real freedom, to allow this love to take me so completely.

Did you have an experience where you recognized with your whole self that you are at one with all-that-is?

Yes, but it was different than what I imagined. It wasn't this big explosion, end of life, end of feeling. It was not like that. It was very simple really. It was this realization that this *me* I have been trying to get rid of is not really a thing. It's not really there so there's nothing to change. It was a very simple realization and an experience of this big love. So much of my life was about getting love, there was so much longing for love. Then to realize that that's what I'm made of, that love is right here. Wow.

It seems like a big shift occurred for you.

Yes, you could say that. But it's not something I have. I don't have anything different than you. We have to be careful with words because we don't want to make this something special. It's not like that. It is a very simple realization that what I have been occupied with my whole life, this me, is just not real. In our trainings or our groups, I see that glimpse of awakening happening to almost everyone. It's not something very rare. But it's about the *becoming* of that. There's a commitment to it, not in the sense that there's a decision, but you fall in love with it so much, it becomes a priority. It becomes everything.

Of course, after that [awakening] were still the habits of this monkey that needed to be addressed, especially in my relating. It was a process of feeling into the beauty and the peace, the love of this awakened dimension. And feeling into the pain of how much schism I felt between this inner realization and what was actually happening in my relationship at the time. I came to a point where I had to find a way where I could bridge this. "OK, I am willing to be alone if I have to, but I will not compromise." I knew I had to find another way to relate, but I didn't have any models. Most often, the way we relate is based on a false sense of separation, that there are two entities coming together to get their needs met.

It was not my primary focus at the time to have any relationship, but I could also see that I'm not destined to live in a cave. I am again and again drawn to relationship. So then I met Arjuna. We had a very interesting meeting, a very sober meeting. There was an attraction but we didn't become lovers for many months because we had this intense dialogue about what we wanted to do. I knew that if I should enter a relationship again, it had to be a relationship that honored and supported my commitment to what I knew to be true in the deepest sense. When I met Arjuna, he had gone through a similar process, so we experienced a deep resonance with each other. It was a kind of a blessing, that start. It was a very conscious exploration.

It wasn't like this overwhelming falling in love kind of thing?

No. That's what happens when you start to have sex. The hormones start going. First we had this very sober dialogue. We wanted to expose all the habits that we knew had come in the way and put them on the table. Usually you just kind of hide them as long as possible [she laughs], and then after some years, they come running back to you. But we put everything on the table.

We also had a very deep dialogue about our vision. I was sharing about what I had come to as my priority, about why I am alive… to live love, to explore, how I can expand more and more in love. That is my deepest commitment. I told him, "If this relationship can support that—good. If not, I'd rather be alone." He shared similar things, so we went through a process of dedicating the relationship to the deeper heart more than anything else. This process is what we are using in our teaching.

Do you want to talk about how you took this real life experience with Arjuna and created the relationship seminars?

Between us, we had done every therapy, every meditation available on this planet, really. We still had not found a way to get rid of the habits, the persona. Most of us have this idea that we can't really love until we get rid of these habits. But love is available in every moment; we just need to loosen our identification with our habits enough so that love can flow through us. We don't have to heal before we can love, simply stop taking our persona so seriously and see that what we are so identified with is a bundle of inherited habits. Who we really are is vast unlimited love, doing its best to be expressed through a human body.

Can we say that habits are conditioning, like protective mechanisms, things that we do to take care of ourselves?

Yes, habits of the persona, habits of the separate identity. So what we explored is how to bridge this being that knows no separation and the persona which is only separation. We don't teach seminars on how to have a happy-ever-after relationship, to learn the right techniques. It's not about that. At the start of each seminar, we guide people back to that original longing of the heart and why you are here on the planet. From there, you ground yourself in that—deeper and deeper, a commitment to that big love, not to the other person.

Then you can create a more fulfilling relationship—not because it is always harmonious or nice, but because it serves that deeper place. A relationship in service to that has a totally different context than a relationship where we are trying to get what we think we lack.

How is it with the two of you in relationship, now that you are practicing this more consciously?

In the relationship I was in before, it was also kind of a spiritual relationship. [She laughs.] I don't know how to call it. But it was an endless process. It was more like you were in it to heal your wounds and process everything, on and on. What's different when we practice this way is that first of all, we always have this reference point. We share our commitment over and over again every morning. This is what life is. This is why I am here. When the habits are coming, we have an agreement to ask, "Is what you're doing now aligned with your deepest commitment?" Then we have ways to get back to love very quickly.

Give me an example of one of those ways. I think that would be helpful.

One way is like theater. One of my habits is that I can be very critical. Then Arjuna can say, "Just keep on doing that, but do it more, like with an accent or like your mother." And then it loses its grip on me, the stickiness is gone. We have an agreement that if we say, "Let's do practice," then whatever one of us suggests, the other one has to do.

We have many, many different tools. Many of them are based on the idea that one sits and holds presence while one is exposing themselves, sharing some habit of the persona. Everything can be welcome—it just doesn't matter anymore. It's the presence that matters. They're very short, it can take five minutes and then we are back in the moment. We have practiced enough that even if we are very upset, there's a strong field of this presence.

It sounds simple.

Love is so simple. I tell you. Love in itself is so simple. But we have an addiction to making things complicated. It's our addiction to mental processes that make things really complicated. To be in an intimate relationship brings up all that stuff. That's one of the reasons why it is attractive to be in a relationship because you get to see yourself, places that you lack practice.

I noticed there are children who live in the house. I imagine that gives you the chance to practice.

Yes, those are my stepsons, they are Arjuna's boys from a previous marriage, and they are here half the time. They bring me face to face with my concept that I can find any kind of resting place where I think I have it all sorted out. Because we are all human beings, growing all the time, there are constantly new things that occur. I'm grateful for that. A part of my spiritual conditioning was that kids would be a distraction to peace. I have learned so much how this peace expands when it gets tested in the fire of real love.

I used to spend half the year in India and half the year preparing for India. I was going to India to contemplate love while I was leaving my family, hurting people. I was not there for Christmas, weddings, or the birth of nephews, all these things. I see in my practice in the last few years that love is not a concept.

I'm sure that this way of looking at the world has a broader impact beyond personal relationships.

Absolutely, the relationship work in itself is a very small vision. I think that even if you get the perfect relationship, it won't be satisfying because it's so small a vision. For us, our relationship is a way to practice big love, and the more we can practice this, the more we can share with others. Then they can also find a way to give it away, because the way you keep connected to the Source, is to keep sharing.

Are there ways that you are now in the world that expresses this big love?

It's mostly about the work with people, in groups—it's all about that. That's my way of sharing. I also work with people one on one, and in my sessions, I give a deep guidance back into who you are. I also work with women and how they can expand their expression throughout the body.

Say more about that.

The term feminine spirituality only makes sense in the context that spirituality has been so dominated by the masculine for thousands of years. It has been about transcending out of here, about the goal, the perfect state that we keep comparing with this present moment. In Eastern traditions especially, the image of spiritual freedom is the void, emptiness. Life in a human body has been seen as a distraction. We have taken that as the reflection of the ultimate truth.

To me, it reflects a kind of a fear of life or a wanting to get out of here, the masculine preference. So what feminine spirituality brings is wholeness or a balance to spirituality, a more embracing quality, a now-based quality. The feminine reminds us that there is no way we can separate the unmanifest ground of being with its manifestation—it is all sacred.

And as you mentioned, it's not only women who are practicing this, but men, too, are staying present in relationship and in family, in life. The feminine sees life as an explosion of all this, it changes form all the time; it doesn't seem to have any end to it. There will not be a time when we have meditated enough, done enough therapy, enough affirmations so that afterwards, life will be smooth, quiet, harmonious. It's just not like that!

So when you start to see life like that, the choice you have is either to resist or to welcome it. When I say "welcome," it's not in an abstract or conceptual way, it's real in that we bring a willingness to stay present with whatever occurs. That's what I mean by embodiment. Awakening itself is just a realization of what's here. It's very much about the practice to embody this presence, how you come back into love even in the midst of whatever is happening.

That's a huge job, for women especially. I meet many women who have had a background with masculine paths, and they see feelings as a distraction to truth. Masculine spirituality has taught us for centuries to get away from feelings, to distance ourselves. Much of the work I do with women is deprogramming of concepts so they can trust their own heart and their own wisdom. We dive completely into feelings, leaving behind the addiction to the story, just staying in the innocent, raw feelings. To totally be with the feelings is being in presence because feelings are made of the same stuff. It comes from the same Source.

Collectively, we are going through a lot of suffering. It's part of my practice, to feel the pain of the world. I can move through very dark places like despair, but I don't create a story around it. When you stay with feeling, the raw essence of feeling, it changes because it's not "velcroed" to the story. Real freedom is having the choice between hopelessness, despair, ecstasy and joy. It doesn't matter. It's just a flavor. That's one of my real passions, to explore these feelings, without resistance. When we resist, we divide it: this or that, this but not that.

How do you see death now?

When I look back into who I am, and I look at that presence, the ground of being that we are, I don't see that it has any end. It has no form, it's not going to die, it's just there. Still, I can feel that this body is going to die, Arjuna's body is going to die, and I can feel the pain of that. I can feel that that's a part of the package of this life. I heard a story where someone said, "Yeah, even when his father died, he didn't cry at all." And that was supposed to be a sign of enlightenment. I would say that's a sign of a very closed person. If that's a goal of spiritual life, you can have it.

Last week I was interviewed on the radio, and this guy was asking me about the pain of separating from his children. He wanted a mantra to take the pain away. I told him, "Even if I had a mantra, I wouldn't wish that for you." I talked about how staying with the feelings allows the jewel of love to reveal itself. Pain is part of the love, the love for his children.

You talked about how many people are experiencing this shift now. I'm wondering what you think is happening.

I'm not so good at making theories of what is happening. I just see more and more people having this realization. But because they are not embodying it or living it fully, they think they have to seek it again. It's more about living whatever realization you have and finding ways to do it now rather than seeking something that you think you don't have.

You had a teacher at one time. Do you still have a teacher now?

Yes. ShantiMayi is still both my teacher and my mentor. The relationship I have with her is one of great love and gratitude. As she says, and I know this, she mirrored my own heart. But still I love her to death for that, even if it's nothing about her.

There was a time it was important to just trust her guidance. It was like, "OK, I have been trying so hard by myself. I will trust you now." Then when she said, "You are love," I trusted it. I put all my energy into investigating that truth. She said exactly what I had been hearing for ten years, but because of this surrender I could really take it in. What I'm teaching now to people is that they don't need to be followers. I'm teaching people to trust their own original longing because I see so much temptation to project onto someone else what you have in your own heart.

Anything else that you feel is really important to add?

The model before us was focused on reaching enlightenment for oneself. Now we can see that every step we take is part of a huge evolutionary wave. For me, that has been the greatest source of freedom, to put all my spiritual practice in the context that it benefits all. I am just a tiny little part of this immense evolutionary wave of consciousness expressing itself in many different ways.

I have no doubt in my heart that my intention and practice will affect something further down the road. I feel a strong sense of responsibility, of urgency, to do whatever I can with whatever love is here. All of what I do, the seminars, the Self-inquiry, my marriage, are dedicated to this big love, the big picture.

ꙮ

Leaving her home in the late afternoon, I reflected on one thing in particular that Chameli said—I need to live whatever realization I have now, rather than seeking something I don't think I have. It was the same message I read in one of the many books I picked up at the beginning of this journey. One of the teachers interviewed said that the belief that some kind of phenomenal change has to happen is actually a postponement preventing you from allowing yourself to just rest in who you are already.

Chameli left me with a sense of urgency. There is no time to waste. Maybe it's because I am almost twice her age. That's sobering. I like to think that I am not in denial about mortality because I experienced it so intimately with the death of my husband. But the fact is—it is easy to forget. That evening after dinner with my friends, I started a letter to Ulli that I continued throughout my trip.

Dear Ulli,

I just realized that I am the very same age as Brian was when he died. It's like a splash of cold water in the face when I really think about that. What would it be like to know that this is my last year? It makes me wonder how Brian felt. Frustrated probably, feeling like he wasted a bunch of time, and wanting more time. I understand him better now that I am a little older and closer to the end of my own life. I don't want to feel frustrated when it's my turn to die. It may be that the beingness that I am is eternal, but this body-mind isn't, and it feels like a precious gift, this life. I don't want to waste it.

Tomorrow I celebrate All Souls' Day with a large group of locals who have been doing ritual together for 30 some years! I guess it's no wonder that I am thinking about death right now since it is the day of the dead. Happy Halloween!

Muni Fluss

Muni was born in Virginia in 1954. She lived in Europe and Africa as a child, returning to the USA in her teenage years. She moved to California during her early 20s where she met her husband and had her two children. Muni now resides with her family in the mountains of British Columbia after emigrating to Canada in 1994.

CHAPTER 4

MUNI FLUSS

We insist that we're asleep,
we insist that we don't know,
we insist that enlightenment lies outside of us,
and so we are always denying all of who we are.

I have always been a very organized, competent person, maybe even a control freak, at least in my younger days. It wasn't like me to forget the directions—again! But that's exactly what happened. I remained calm, knowing that somehow I would find my way to Muni's sister's house in Berkeley where she was staying after the all-woman's retreat. I made several phone calls until I got her home phone number where she and her husband live in Nelson, British Columbia. While driving down the freeway towards the Bay Area, Muni's husband finally called me back with the directions. It was a good lesson in the mind's limitations.

Muni was waiting for me on the second storey of a small, old apartment complex in the heart of the city. We set up outside in the courtyard garden at a picnic table. Muni was wrapped in a paisley shawl, and when she saw me looking a little chilled, she insisted on getting me a matching shawl.

She spoke softly, as her name suggests. Adya gave her the name; Muni means the Silent One, and it suited her well. I had to make sure the microphone was close enough to pick up her gentle voice. At one time, we were interrupted by a screaming siren, and later, by a neighbor yelling in a nearby apartment. But nothing seemed to disturb the field of serenity Muni created.

☙❧

Share with us a little bit about your story so we can understand how you got to where you are now.

I was born in Lexington, Virginia, to a father who was a diplomat. My family and I lived overseas in a few different countries in Europe, and in Africa from the time I was 2 until age 14. My Dad died when I was 14, and we moved back to the United States. I was close to my Dad. He was someone I could talk with, being a philosopher, author, theologian, and educator. He was good at asking questions but not giving any answers, something like Self-inquiry.

After he died and we moved back to the USA, I was quite miserable. I had no one to relate to who understood me the way my father did. I had a hard time adjusting to this culture, felt imprisoned by it, by my family, by everything. I like to tell the truth, and people didn't want to hear it. I was told I was crazy.

I tried to kill myself and ended up in a mental institution. It was actually the perfect place for me. In that space, I was able to be quiet and have the solitude I enjoy as well as being outside the normal societal pressures and constraints. The people in that institution were there because they were very different people. I had always felt different, too, like an alien on this planet. I didn't fit in, especially in a diplomatic family. In a diplomatic family, everything is supposed to look good, you're supposed to put on a good face but not say what's really going on. That was so frustrating for me. I don't think I really wanted to be here, not in bodily form. I enjoyed the formless too much. So I got quite a jolt as a way to let me know that I *am* actually here, and I was meant to be here. I was abused as a child emotionally and sexually by my brother. That went on for many years, off and on, on and off. It really wasn't addressed; it was something you didn't talk about. I told my mother, and it was, "Shh, don't tell your father. I'll handle it." So I didn't tell my Dad, and I handled it the best way I could.

Can I ask you how the early abuse was resolved for you? And please, feel free to say that you are uncomfortable talking about it.

OK. Thanks. My brother is still alive. Richard lives here in Oakland. After I got out of the mental institution and saw Richard, he was still behaving in ways that were inappropriate and would be considered molestation. The message I received in the hospital as well as from society was that it was not OK to tell the truth, so I didn't know how to respond to him. How do you deal with it if you can't tell the truth? I just let it be for the time being. I did whatever I needed to do, which was not to be alone with him.

He disappeared after a time. I was in my 20s living in California when I got a call from Richard in Salt Lake City. Apparently, he had moved there, and this was the first contact that he was making with any member of the family. I guess he felt he could talk to me and wanted me to come. I decided to go, but not alone, so my sister and I went. We were sitting with Richard, and he asked me point blank, "Did you try to kill yourself because of what I did?" And I said, "Oh my God, no." He thought he was to blame. Out of that question came what I thought was a wonderful, intimate conversation. But he was also drinking. We went back to his apartment where my sister and I were staying. I went to sleep that night, and I could hear him alone in the other room—more of a continuing molestation kind of thing. It was verbal at this point, and I was completely outraged. How could he do this after that conversation?

I said to my sister, "Can you believe this?!" She was pretending to be asleep, but I knew she could hear me. I didn't want to ignore Richard's behavior or hope it would go away. I wanted to address it directly, especially after our open conversation. There was some fear as well as anger.

So we packed our bags, put them by the front door, and then we walked over to him in the living room where he was lying on the couch naked in a very inappropriate manner and asked, "What is going on here? This is not OK. Either we have a talk now and speak the truth or we walk out the door never to see you again. It's the truth or nothing. I'm not going to be here for anything else."

He knew we were sincere and began to open up to us. Simply put, he said, "I love you, and this is the only way I know how to express it." I got it. I could really hear the truth in that. I responded that I understood that love was definitely present but was being expressed in a very inappropriate way. I guess it was right then that I forgave him. Adya [Adyashanti] has this beautiful description of forgiveness: "Let it be." And that was what happened. I got the truth and then let it be. So I guess that was the resolution.

He shot himself in 1984. He survived, the bullet is still in his brain, but he's paralyzed on one side of his body. That can appear like a very tragic thing. Who knows, it's really not for me to say. But I can say that when I'm with him I do love who he is, no matter how his life appears.

What was it about being here in this culture back when you were younger that was so hard for you?

It was about knowing God. Why can't I meet God, here in the world? If I can't meet God here, then let me do away with this body. I know God here in this formless place, but where is God in form? I had this incessant drive to connect with someone about this. I was asking people, "Let me share this with you, do you know what I'm talking about?" People would respond, "You can't go around talking like that. That's crazy." Some of what I was saying was *satsang* material even back then. I couldn't explain it because it doesn't make sense to the mind.

Often in *satsang* circles, there is the memory of when awakening took place. It had a date and time. I couldn't relate to this. There was a group of teachers meeting with Adya, just a small gathering, and they were talking about the experience of their awakening. I said to the group, "I can't relate. I can't give a date and time. Maybe I'm in the wrong place here." Adya just looked at me and said, "That's because you came in awake." It shot through me like an arrow because it was true, and I knew it was true. I can't make any sense out of that, but I do know it's true.

Is it a unique experience to be born awake?

I don't think so. Not that it means anything significant in any kind of way. But before I knew that, it hadn't dawned on me that people were not aware of their own Source. I thought everyone was just pretending. It was a real eye-opener. It explained so much about some of the behaviors of people that I had not understood before.

Let's go back to the hospital and how you got out.

I was 16 when I tried to kill myself, and I was about 22 when I got out. I wasn't in the hospital the whole time. The longest I stayed was maybe a year. In the hospital, they would say, "You have to tell us what's going on here or we can't help you." Eventually I came to the realization, "Do I really need help? I don't know. These people seem kinda crazy here." That's what it felt like. I realized, "I'm not crazy. The world, society, people, the whole set-up is crazy." When I realized that, I went underground.

It wasn't OK to be telling the truth at that time, at least in those circles. People weren't going around saying this kind of stuff. You had to be from India or have some kind of background that authenticated this kind of inquiry. I have a little journal I wrote that I kept in the hospital. I guess I was trying to make every effort to explain the unexplainable.

[Later, Muni shared the following from her journal written in 1970 at the age of 16 when she was in the mental institution. "I live in a box, I live surrounded by walls. We all do. There was a time when there were no walls. Just the SELF. LOVING. It's like a sea, a clouded sea, which is not water but love and knowledge and happiness. As I grew older, I developed those walls, they were a defense mechanism. I began to notice other walls and realized that I could not see past them. When the walls close you in, happiness is also closed in and cannot be completed. I'm afraid of being

closed in completely but also afraid of complete freedom."]

No one seemed able or interested in hearing what I was saying. So I decided, "OK, I don't want to live in a hospital. I want to get out of here." There were people who had been in the facility for 10 to 12 years, and I didn't want to do that because I liked being in nature too much to remain locked up. I remember making a conscious decision to say what it was the key holders wanted to hear. I did that and got out.

When I was in University in DC just before and during the hospital days, I studied music theory, voice, and piano. When I moved to California after being in the hospital, I was no longer involved with music and no longer had a voice. It was something I left behind in order to get out of the confinement of the hospital. It is interesting that I let it go. I didn't sing for a long time after that. I used to love to sing. [She has tears.] It touches me because it's still true. I love to sing. I love to give voice to the truth. And I do that now.

Then I discovered yoga. I went to a class and fell completely in love with yoga. Yoga is one of the many branches of the same tree. It all leads to unity. After the first class, I knew there was something there, and I kept coming back to the Berkeley Yoga Room. I started yoga in 1980, began teaching in 1989, and stopped teaching three or four years ago. Yoga was a beautiful way for me to really immerse myself in this body form. I had been resisting this embodiment. I was saying, "I don't want to be here." Life kept saying, "You are here." With yoga as a tool, being in the body was something I came to appreciate.

Tell me how you met your husband.

As I was going through the prerequisites for nursing school in a micro-biology class, I met Larry in the first class. I was sitting near the doorway, with a huge cast on from recent knee surgery. Larry walked in, and there was immediate intense eye contact. We actually *saw* each other. I felt a recognition and extreme gratitude as well as excitement. He sat down next to me and asked, "So what happened to your leg?" He was just right out there, with nothing hidden. He's a helluva guy. It was definitely an immediate click. I really liked the perfume, you can say, although he didn't wear any. I was drawn to the radiance.

At the time I met Larry, I was fed up with men and not looking for a relationship. He asked me out, I agreed, but he broke the date. Initially the cancellation played into my annoyance with men. He had a sincere reason for breaking the date and asked me again. I felt drawn to him. It felt "right," so I agreed. I am still with Larry, have been since 1981.

When you think about Larry now, what is the quality in the relationship that you love?

That he's real. If he has to burp, he burps. And if he's embarrassed about burping, then you could read it all over his face. If he's trying to hold something in, it becomes very obvious. He is so beautiful as a mate because he calls me on any kind of bullshit that I might come up with, as do my children. I so appreciate that. He's not a spiritual seeker, so the kind of conversations that I might have desired—the kind of conversations I was looking for as a teenager and as a young adult before I met Adya—I couldn't really have that conversation with Larry as readily as I wanted. He didn't speak the same kind of language, but we could easily share all the stuff about our lives. I shared about the hospital days, and he shared about his brother who is mentally ill. We were like this [crosses her fingers]. We touched hearts; it was the outline of the one heart that we were embracing together.

You didn't marry someone you could share the spiritual path with. So how do you negotiate that as a couple?

He does share it. To say that he's not a spiritual seeker does not mean that he's not *here* also. He may not dialogue or have the words in this way, even though he could. To him, it's not the way. He's not comfortable with it. He's been at Adya's intensives. Adya came and stayed at our house when he was in Canada, and Larry had conversations with Adya, but Larry would hate doing a retreat. He's extremely open and supportive. Whenever I get niggly and want to have one of my conversations, he's available, but he's available in a very appropriate way. When he can hear it, great. When he doesn't want to hear it, he tells me. It's always a teaching, whatever response comes.

We don't have to live in some fantasy of what a spiritual life should look like. It's not separate from our humanity. The most holy place I have ever been is in nature. Nature is *my* nature. There's shit in the woods. You might just step in bear poop around where I live, and I like that. It fertilizes the ground. You can say the same with my family and my home. It is really fertile ground for the growing of everything that wants to blossom and all of life. Why exclude anything? The thing that's been so difficult in this story of mine is that anything that wants to be excluded really hurts.

What do you do with strong feelings?

Just let them be. I'm growing into who I am, all of who I am. Once I said to Adya, "You must have made a mistake in asking me to teach," buying into the thought that awakened, enlightened people don't behave the way in which I do. "No, I didn't make a mistake," he said. So here [she places her hand on her heart], anger arises, sadness arises, there's a touching of the heart. The human being is here, it doesn't want to be excluded and neither do any of these emotions. So are they a problem? No. We are meant to feel.

Physically in this body, I have two hands. When they come together and embrace, you can really take the full bow into the heart, the heart of the matter. It's in my kitchen when I'm making dinner, and everybody wants something from me at the same time, and the dog's barking because someone rang the doorbell, and the phone's ringing, and it's too much, and it's just got to STOP! It's right there in the nitty-gritty—that is the most beautiful place.

In the midst of an argument with Larry where I'm screaming inside with frustration, there's also this amazing laughter that goes "What am I doing?!" and loving it, loving it and him. Why would I want to leave that out? Why would I want to leave anger out? Why would I want to leave any of it out? What's a mistake here? [She takes a deep breath.] You really got me on a roll. [She laughs.]

Yeah, you like that part. It's juicy. Let's talk about your two teenage daughters. You said they were teachers for you. Tell us more about that.

When I am acting the mothering role, and it's not really coming from spontaneity or any depth of Self, they call me on it. They demand authenticity, thank God. They show me the gaps in myself.

Give me an example.

Sasha is the oldest, and she's a very quiet person, she's very much an observer. From the minute she was born, even from the time of conception, she was very OK in herself. She's not what "social" usually looks like. I really love Sasha, and so sometimes I want to do something that looks like reaching out: "Tell me what's going on in your life," or "How is school?" She doesn't really talk about it. When I press her on it, she gets mad, "I don't want to talk about it," or she gets snippy. This is an incredible teaching because it is none of my business, and aren't we already connected?

One day I pressed her, and she pretty much said, "Screw off, Mom." We sat down, we were both teary eyed. I think it was my birthday, actually. I felt I had reached out to connect and been rejected. It's hard for her to put emotions into words sometimes, and what part of me was it that was asking her to? She sat in my lap and with tears in her eyes she said so simply, "I don't really like 'doing' it like that. I already feel like we're connected, and

I don't need to talk to you like that." She was reflecting such truth, teaching the silence that I already know. So she really calls me on it. Even the words she uses, "I'm not like that." In other words, "That's not my form."

Kaila has a beautiful voice, and singing is an important part of her life. In her childhood years, she was totally unconcerned with the world, just reveling in the joy of being here and loving everything. These teenage times, not uncommonly, have been kind of challenging for her. It has sometimes been a struggle for her to get up and sing her solos, to let her voice move freely. One evening she was having a difficult time and asked to talk with me. She had been looking on my website and was now asking to engage in *satsang*.

We sat together in my bedroom and explored some of the questions that she had been pondering. Questions like… "What is this that is so deeply present and doesn't seem possible for me to express?" "I don't seem to be able to connect. Is it me?" "What's really going on? How do I be this depth of being that I know that I am?" I just listened, curious what was there in front of me. It is funny how when you really listen to someone they begin to really listen to themselves also. And then there it is, whatever it is that wants to be seen is seen.

Do you give satsang *in Nelson where you live?*

I started offering *satsang* in Nelson after Adya talked to me about teaching. I felt awkward about it. I had nothing to substantiate what I was imparting, no explanations. It is just the direct experience of *being* that is imparted. It is not about reiterating scripture, or representing what someone else taught, or copying someone else's way of being. There is no *right* way of being. I was hesitant to teach, a fear reminiscent of those hospital days. I wasn't sure that it was OK to speak the truth. I thought it meant I had to do something or be someone other than myself. Adya was speaking to *being* and was inviting that to give voice to itself once again. It was an invitation to come out of the closet. Adya gave one main pointer: it doesn't have to look any particular way. This continues to be more and more true. Literally you can say I have not been *finding*, but *freeing* up my voice since meeting Adya. I stuffed it to leave the hospital. I once asked him why he asked me to give *satsang* and he said, "Sometime you'll know." Now I know.

Do you think your experience of death at an early age had a particularly strong influence on your interest in the spiritual?

It had a big impact on me. I was really curious about it. When I saw my father die, I saw how beautiful the release "home" was, into the formlessness. I didn't want to do the form thing. When I tried to kill myself as a teenager, I almost succeeded. I've been really afraid of death since I tried to kill myself. When I woke up in intensive care, and it actually dawned on me that I was the one who tried to kill myself, it was a shock. It had seemed fine, from a formless perspective, you could say. But from a human standpoint, one thinks of murderers, and one locks their doors at night. Here I was the one who had attempted murder.

My Mom had a slow death, ten years… well, all her life, I guess. You're dying all the time. It's the same for all of us. A long, slow death our whole lives, unless we wake up to our own births as well. The events around my mother's death are interesting. We brought my mother home to my sister's house, and all gathered there. I flew from California with my babies. My mother was not someone you could really talk to in the way I wanted to talk to her, but on her deathbed she was very open to non-verbal communication. You know, everyone is open to presence, not necessarily wanting to talk about it or acknowledge it, but everyone is open to it. She was especially so at that time.

I brought Kaila who was three months to my mother's bedside. This was their first meeting. Mom's eyes lit up when she saw Kaila. Mom had been moving in and out of orientation. I put Kaila on Mom's chest, and she was so touched. I couldn't leave Kaila there long, she started wailing. Mom asked, "What's going on? What is that sound? Somebody's dying." It sounded like Kaila was dying, the way she was wailing. "I know somebody is dying, who is it? Is it Aunt Polly? Is it Uncle Bill? Who is it?" I blurted out, "Mom, you're the one who is dying." She said, "Oh, thank God. Take this oxygen mask off and let's get on with it."

The exhalation is obviously the last thing that happens when you die. Mom took 15 minutes to let the breath go... a long time between inhalation and exhalation. It got to be a kind of joke. Here we all were, breathing out with her. Then we would all burst into tears, thinking she was gone. She would take another breath in, and we would all laugh. That's very much how life is, life and death. The inhalation—everyone is joyous and it's great. Then, on the exhalation, there is this grief and sense of loss. And then there's another inhalation. [She laughs.]

I was at the appointment with a friend when she found out she had a terminal disease and not long to live. There's a ripeness when people get that kind of death sentence which we get the moment we are born, but we haven't taken it in fully. It opens us to all the potential of what we're pregnant with. That's *satsang*. *Satsang* is a place where people come to die. And in that death, we can be born to now. Not born again, just more born, more fully embodied, and then let go again.

All over the place, things are dying, things are being born. Whenever we try to grab onto anything, we are hanging onto an illusion. *Satsang* provides the arena to simply be present as does every minute of every day.

Before we close, I want to ask whether or not you see a particular role that women teachers have at this time.

Yes, to speak up, to speak out to all women and to all people. It was very well spoken at the recent inauguration of the Sangha Sisters retreats. In this circle of women, one of the things I so enjoyed was the different forms in which it came through. Hearing the different flavors gave me an opportunity to birth a fuller voice. There was the "ah-ha" that any form is OK, every form is OK. That's what women have the voice to speak. Women actually bear the baby. Men impregnate, and women give the physical birth to all diversity of form.

We insist that we're asleep. We insist that we're not awake. We insist that we don't know. We insist that enlightenment lies outside of us, and so we are always denying all of who we are. We have this horrible denial addiction going on. Everyone. But women especially have over time and history been a little confined, a little contained. I think that's changing. I think this book is an awesome opportunity to give voice to what the feminine flavor has to offer.

ಬಂಞ

Muni walked me back to the camper where Kiva was waiting for his walk. She wanted to show me on a city map where I could go for a little stroll. Being a country girl herself, she knew that was important. Not long later, I was standing on a green hill on the edge of Berkeley watching the sun set into the ocean.

I pondered what Muni had said about her mother's "long, slow death, her whole life," and took note of this possibility "unless we wake up to our own births as well." That night, I stayed on a residential street near a friend's apartment where I parked the camper. I cooked dinner and continued my letter to Ulli:

Do you ever regret not having children? It's only now in midlife that I feel the loss of not having any kids. I was too busy before enjoying my freedom, maybe even thinking that someday I might get around to it. Now there are practical matters that come up, like who is going to inherit the house I built or what will become of all the journals I have saved since high school. Without children in the picture, there is no pretending about the fate of all this stuff, the symbols of the personality. It makes it more obvious how temporary this all is.

When Brian died, I waited eight months before getting to the difficult task of going through all his memorabilia, digging through the attic, setting aside a few things for his daughter. But even his daughter didn't want all of the trophies, newspaper clippings, the photos. I felt a little guilty, unceremoniously dumping the boxes into the dumpster. The sum total of a life in the trash can. I remember thinking that all this stuff is clearly not what is important. I'm reflecting on this because of what Muni said in my interview today about needing to birth ourselves or else we just die a long, slow death.

I suppose it all comes back to the big question, why are we here? What is life all about? I used to think there was some meaning to life. But that's not the point now. The question now becomes, what remains, what doesn't die at the moment of death, what is real?

Dorothy Hunt

Dorothy was born in 1943, has practiced psychotherapy since 1965 and is the founder of the San Francisco Center for Meditation and Psychotherapy. She is a teacher in the spiritual lineage of Adyashanti, serves as Spiritual Director of Moon Mountain Sangha, Inc. and is the author of *Only This!* Dorothy is also the editor of *Love: A Fruit Always in Season,* and a contributing author to both *The Sacred Mirror: Non-Dual Wisdom and Psychotherapy,* and *Listening from the Heart of Silence: Non-Dual Wisdom and Psychotherapy, Vol. 2.* Dorothy lives with her husband in San Francisco; she's a mother and a grandmother.

CHAPTER 5

DOROTHY HUNT

This that we are is a mystery.
Everything is both an invitation to and an expression of
that mystery.
There's nothing that isn't That.
It's all That. This is That.

The next morning I woke up refreshed. I had slept well, which was remarkable since I wasn't used to streetlights, the sounds of the city, the crooked angle of my bed. A real contrast from the quiet of the "loneliest highway." I knew it would be a long day, driving across the Bay Bridge into the heart of downtown San Francisco, then heading out of the city again and south on Highway 1. From the moment I decided to bring the camper, I knew the hardest part would be driving on the busy streets, and I was a little anxious about it; more intimidating than driving in a snowstorm!

However, the pre-stress was unjustified in relation to the actual event, as is so often the case. I always think of going to the dentist to remind me of that truth. The drive into San Francisco was magical, like coming into the Emerald City. I admired the architecture of the bridge, awed by the sheer feat of its construction. I could appreciate the beauty of the skyscrapers, the manmade-ness of it all. I flowed easily along with the traffic, took all the right turns and even found a good parking space for the big rig near Dorothy's office.

I opened the combination to the little door which led upstairs to the second storey of an old building above an Italian restaurant. After greeting me in the shared reception area at the top of the stairs, Dorothy led me to her office, filled with light from a south-facing window. Big plants thrived. There was a couch, a desk that was mostly empty except for a small Buddha statue, and two overstuffed chairs facing each other, everything in its place.

Dorothy was dressed professionally in a brown top and pants, a red scarf and red loafers to match.

It was her eyes that got my attention… dark, warm, deep. Just like the eyes of my husband after he died. There was nothing to filter or obstruct the experience of the eternal, once the individual me-ness of Brian was gone.

Dorothy's soft gaze put me at ease. It was a bit of a relief since my email conversations with Dorothy were the most challenging of any of the women I contacted. Though gentle, she was direct. She wanted to know all about the project, whether I had been published before, what was my focus, who else had agreed to be included. Dorothy is a psychotherapist and a writer herself, so it's not surprising that she would take such an interest in the specifics of the project. When preparing for the interview, I read her contribution in a book about non-dual psychotherapy. Articulate and clear, I knew that her interview would be the same.

෨෦෬

I think it's a good idea to start with childhood, to describe any early experiences that really stand out.

The first thing I would say is it seems to me that the mystery is always moving. It's not an individual who finds the mystery, but it's the mystery that expresses itself as a unique body-mind. The truth you imagine you're searching for is always right here; it never has been anywhere else. The idea of finding something, or going towards it, certainly is the experience of the so-called spiritual seeker, but I think the seeker and the movement is simply the expression of the mystery.

With that in mind, I can tell you that probably the defining moment of the so-called personal life was the death of my mother when I was a child. It really threw open the door to the questions of life, death, what's it all about. I wanted to know who was this God who could give life and take it away? I grew up in a Protestant household. My Grandpa was a Methodist minister. Religion wasn't a huge part of our family life but definitely part of the background. So that was actually the beginning of a more conscious search for answers to big questions.

How old were you?

I had just turned 12. My mother died the day after Christmas, and her birthday the following year was going to be on Easter Sunday. In a very deep and innocent childhood faith, I prayed every day she would be resurrected on Easter like Jesus. I had read in the Bible that if you had faith the size of a mustard seed you could move mountains, and I knew that my faith was bigger than a mustard seed. So I believed in this possibility on some level.

On another level, of course, there was a reality there, but someplace I was completely convinced she would be resurrected on her Easter birthday. I was very excited when that day came, and I remember setting a place for her at the table for breakfast. Of course, the resurrection did not happen as I had hoped, and that was a huge disillusionment, a child's disillusionment with God. But that didn't keep me from being very interested in the question: who is this God that gives life and takes it away?

When a parent dies, you actually lose both parents for awhile—the one who died and also the surviving parent to grief. I had a tree seat my Dad built in this apple tree in our backyard, and I sat in that apple tree a lot. I loved to sit in that tree prior to her death, too, but especially afterward. I never felt really lonely in nature. It was somehow in the presence of the tree and nature that I could just be. It was, and still is, a great part of how the so-called spiritual dimension reveals itself within itself.

Now we could fast forward through college, meeting my husband, getting married, still on the so-called search, but not nearly so much as living a normal kind of life without deeply searching for anything through many, many years. I started meditating at least 30 years ago. At that point I was married with two children, and my husband and I had moved from the

Midwest to San Francisco.

I was in the Christian tradition, and meditation wasn't something that was taught at all in the church I went to. I read a little book, however, that said if you wanted to meditate and you were Christian, you could meditate on a passage of the scripture, so I chose: "Be still and know that I am God," Psalms 46:10. Every day for a number of years, that's what I would sit with, and I really got to know every one of those words. I would break it up; what is it to "be"? What is it to "be still"? What is it to "be still and know"?

Then one day in my meditation, it became very clear I was supposed to be doing something with Mother Teresa of Calcutta. I had no idea her sisters, the Missionaries of Charity, were in San Francisco. They had just opened a house there, so I called them. While it was very new for me to move from such a mysterious place, I later found out that it was the way people came to them all the time.

The sister I spoke with said to me, "Do you have a car? We've just been in the chapel praying for someone who has a car." I said, "Yes, I have a car." "Are you free on Fridays?" I answered, "Well, as a matter of fact, I don't work on Fridays." I showed up not knowing at all what we were going to be doing. It was a complete leap of faith. We went down to the Tenderloin, which is our city's skid row, and visited with the homeless people on the street, giving them sandwiches and coffee and just talking.

I had been working as a psychotherapist for awhile at that point, so when I would encounter the homeless, many of whom were addicted or mentally ill, my mind activity revolved around questions such as, "Have you tried this clinic?" or "What about medication?" The sisters in their very sweet way let me know there was nothing wrong with what I did for a living, but that wasn't why we were there. We were there just to give love in the moment with no expectation for change, and that was a great, great teaching.

It was the beginning of the teaching of true nature, but of course, I wasn't calling it "true nature" at the time. Our true nature shows up for what is here and doesn't require anything to be different. That is what the sisters were inviting me to experience—more than experience, just to be.

One thing I learned from Mother Teresa is something I have never forgotten. It was how powerful and transformative love can be in just a single moment. The first time I met her, she held my face in her hands, and there was such presence and such love, I can't really describe it in words. But there was a knowing that a single moment can make a change. That was her teaching to me.

After maybe ten years of being involved with the Missionaries of Charity, it was clear there was another movement happening. I had an interest in Buddhism and had occasionally gone to retreats with Thich Nhat Hanh. In 1994, I had a dream that changed my life. Ramana Maharshi's face appeared in a dream, but I didn't know who it was at the time. In the dream I was so taken, so drawn, by those eyes that I just knew I had to find who this was. I knew nothing about him consciously, but he appeared in the dream with such profound beauty and silence that I had to find out.

Later, I realized I had bought a book, *The Spiritual Teachings of Ramana Maharshi*, some years before. You know how you can buy books and put them on the shelf, you forget you even bought them, and you don't read them? I began reading the book, and it was really hard going. There were all these Sanskrit terms I had no knowledge of, and yet I persevered because it felt like I was reading the deepest truth I had ever come across up until that point in my life.

I was reading the book on an airplane one day while flying back from being with my daughter who was then in graduate school in the Midwest. The air became very turbulent, the plane was bouncing and shaking, people were "white-knuckling" it. And a thought just came, "Let me see if I can experience what Ramana Maharshi is talking about in this moment." In whatever way the mystery moves, there was immediately a sense of everything dropping away, and I was just being the vast mystery itself. I had this clear sense that if my body should die, nothing would change. I would still be who I was in that moment.

That was the first *conscious* taste of my true nature, this mystery. At the time, of course, I imagined it was something *I* had done, but now I see it from the other direction. The whole experience was just life moving. But that first "taste," while reading Ramana's book, made it very clear there was something in this man that was calling to me. I began to do Self-inquiry as Ramana taught, not as an intellectual practice, but the question began asking itself, "Who am I?" "Who's sitting here talking?" "Who's looking at her reflection in the shop window as she walks by?" "Who is thinking?"

I never wanted a guru. I always felt sorry for people who were looking for one. I experienced an internal, accessible God I could talk to, be comforted by, the one I had found in the apple tree. I always thought, "Why go to a person when you can have God?" But in the eyes of Ramana, there was such presence. At one point I asked the eyes, "Are you my guru?" The immediate response back was, "The Self is your guru." I knew it was true. The guru simply represents your own deep truth.

That inquiry of "Who am I?" doesn't ever give us an answer. It stops the mind. When the mind stops even for a few seconds, our true nature reveals itself because it's always been right here; it's never been anywhere else. It's the mind's continual thought of separation, the thought called "me" that makes it seem harder to taste it, to really know in your own experience this is who you are, this incredible mystery. It's right here, just right here prior to the mind's thoughts.

After about three years of the inquiry, "Who am I?" the moment came leaving no doubt whatsoever. I happened to be looking up in a circle of trees when there was an overwhelming sense of recognition of who I am and who I had always been. I needed no one to confirm that experience. There was no doubt whatsoever that I was what I was looking for, and I was everything else as well—the trees, the earth, the sky, all of life, nature in its fullness—which isn't all good and bliss. It is everything, dark and light, every set of opposites.

You use the word "recognition." Sometimes I have heard the word "awakening" for this moment of awareness. Is there any difference?

Some people have bells and whistles experiences, and some people are awakened to their nature in a much quieter way, without this kind of experience. Maybe they just came in that way. But to recognize our true nature is the same as awakening to it. It's recognizing, "This has been here all along. I just never noticed before. I was busy doing other things."

For me, the initial moment of recognition was more like bells and whistles. It was one of those experiences filled with tears and laughter and dancing and lying on the ground for such gratitude for the moment, feeling like if I died the next day, I would die complete. That was the power and profundity for me of that experience. After that, I never could forget. But what it clearly, clearly showed is there was no [separate] one to enlighten. There was no one to awaken. There was a sense of everything being fine as it is. For me at that point, there was a detachment that had not yet turned intimate. That's where Adyashanti comes into the story.

It seems like many people I have spoken with have described this one moment as a reference point, but that is not the end of the story.

It's just the beginning as it turns out. What we would call the awakening experience is just the beginning of learning to live from the felt sense of understanding more consciously, the beginning of what we might call the embodiment process. Usually, for most people, awakening is waking up out of the relative, out of the personal, into the Absolute. The sense is I am not my body, not my mind. I am That which is really an eternal mystery that cannot be defined.

The embodiment process is being able to come back into the relative world and to see the whole of existence, including the very movement of one's body and mind, is really the same essence. We go from "I am That" to "I am This" and of course, it's the same thing, but the flavor is different. I have been incredibly fortunate to have been with a teacher whom I would call an embodiment teacher, and that's Adyashanti.

After the experience of realization among the trees, I really felt the seeking had ended. I had been writing to Ramesh Balsekar prior to that time, and he blessedly wrote to me on a few occasions. I would write reams to him, and he would write these tiny little handwritten notes of a few lines back, always asking me, "Who is the questioner? Find out who is the questioner." At one point he gave me one bit of advice: "Forget the questions!"

I had never called him, we had never met, but we had had this correspondence, and I called him to tell him about the awakening experience. His response was very matter of fact, "Yes, yes, everything is quiet now. So how is your family?" It was what every good teacher should do at that moment. You don't make a big to-do about it because really, you have discovered nothing. It's only the mind thinking you were something else, but you've always been what you are.

What happened next was an ease of accessing the Absolute that would come from simply asking, "Who am I?" There was an ease of stopping thought and accessing the emptiness. In the Buddhist tradition, you would be encouraged to let go of the raft when it has taken you to the other shore. But I didn't. I kept the raft, the question, "Who am I?" That inquiry, in a sense, kept taking me out of life, out of the body, there was not an intimacy with life here and now.

In the Buddhist tradition, that would be termed "getting stuck in emptiness." I saw the Divine in every eye I looked at, and it felt like the Divine was looking back at itself. That never went away, but what I would say now is the emptiness wasn't "dancing."

Realizing "I am That" is coming halfway around the circle. It's really an important thing. "That" can't embody as "This" consciously if there's no recognition you and all things are this mystery of being. As I look back—I didn't recognize it at the time—I was hanging out in emptiness with some degree of detachment. I was still involved in life and seeing clients and loving my kids. Life was happening, but in terms of what I now know to be possible which is ever-deepening, there was something stuck.

In 2001, Adyashanti and I were both speakers at the same conference on Non-Dual Wisdom and Psychotherapy. He was the keynote speaker in the evening, and I had been the first speaker in the afternoon. He had come to my talk and I, of course, stayed for his. Literally, the minute he opened his mouth, there was some recognition there was a transmission happening that was needed. How transmission occurs is a mystery, but the experience for me was light and energy coming from his third eye that met something in me, and I knew I needed to be with him in some way.

Life delivers many surprises. There was a retreat that many of my friends had been invited to go on with Adyashanti at a place in the Eastern Sierras. I had never gone to see Adyashanti before. I didn't go to see Gangaji or Bryon Katie or any of the other teachers who were teaching in this area either. I wasn't seeking anything. But the very next day after meeting Adyashanti, someone dropped out of the retreat, and I was invited. I had to move heaven and earth to go on that retreat the following week. My husband wasn't too happy I was racing off with so little notice to this retreat as he was in the middle of a trial, he is an attorney, and we had houseguests. From that retreat until this very moment, Adyashanti has been a living buddha to me and a living example of truth. In him I have seen how emptiness dances spontaneously with so much love and so much devotion to itself.

How did your life change after the retreat?

Shortly after I met Adyashanti in July of 2001, many things began to fall apart. In September, 9/11 happened. My son worked near the World Trade Center, and we didn't know if he was alive or not for many hours after the explosions. The next month, I was diagnosed with breast cancer and had surgery. What I now know is that this awakeness we are, when it's actually moving completely through the cycle—not just waking itself up out of the body but coming back into the body—it comes back for everything. This love comes back for everything, every single thing that has not been touched by its own love, its own truth. It comes back to liberate itself— whatever we haven't seen or met, whatever we've rejected, whatever is our karma that hasn't been accepted.

That's where having a teacher like Adya is a great help because there isn't a lot written or spoken about what I call the "blessed mess of embodiment." We think we've lost something because all this upheaval is happening, but we're not losing anything except our illusions. There's enough consciousness moving that we can now meet whatever and whoever we've been in relationship with outside of the full truth.

It's at this point people's relationships often fall apart, people's bodies often fall apart, people's psyches seem like they're falling apart. I see it now from the perspective of being a teacher, on the other side, but it's at this point there's often a sense of great failure which is, of course, exactly the point. It's the joy of utter defeat. The defeat is of the mind that imagines it's going to be in control or that enlightenment will deliver "goodies" to a "me."

The way this embodiment process works is we're invited to actually just *be* this presence, this love, this acceptance, that liberates everything, not because we're tying to fix something. When we're present to life as it is in ourselves, our bodies, our minds, our emotions, our partners, our children— when we're actually able to simply be here with what's here, transformation begins to happen. And it's not our doing. The mind doesn't know how to be intimate. It doesn't know how to love. It doesn't know how to surrender. It's very good at figuring out things like how to fix your bicycle or car or maybe put a man into space.

Or how to get to Union and Gough [the location of Dorothy's office].

Absolutely. I'm happy I have a mind when I am losing my memory as fast as it seems to be going. I appreciate that I still have a mind. It's just that the mind is doing what minds do: it separates, categorizes, interprets, and tells us what we like and don't like. It's conditioning, fed into it like you would put information into a computer—that's all it knows how to spit back. That's why in the spiritual life, we have an urge to look into the unknown. The mind doesn't really have a clue. The mind can't possibly understand how you can be at peace when life in the moment isn't peaceful, or how you can be enjoying an experience of tumult in some way—just the sheer experience of life as it is.

Can you be specific and talk about how you experienced the tumult of breast cancer?

I experienced it with a tremendous amount of help, support, and love from my husband and our family, for one thing, and from friends, some of whom had also been through an experience with cancer. Day to day, no one was more supportive than my husband. His strength and presence beside me was an incredible gift and an enormous comfort.

Adyashanti was also a great, great help. He was possibly one of the only people in my life who never met my situation or my fear with fear. I specifically avoided being with people who I knew were very fearful because fear invites fear. It's not that I didn't have fear, or that I was denying my own fear. It was just that what was most helpful to me in trying to make decisions about what to do, what not to do, and all the rest was to actually be in my own experience and to be around people who were not afraid of illness or death.

I had surgery, and I had never had surgery before. I hadn't been in the hospital apart from the birthing experience. Adya often speaks about how This that we are wouldn't miss this life. That's what it's here for; it showed up for that. We apparently want a human experience, right? We often say we are humans looking for the Divine, but the Divine is here having a human experience, not just for the good part but the whole of it.

I had such a sense of that as I lay waiting for the surgery to begin. There was a complete curiosity. It was a very novel experience. It wasn't at all the way I had imagined. There was no fear in the moment. I had been incredibly afraid before and there was fear afterwards, but in that moment there was just this curiosity about things. I was fortunate in that the cancer was not invasive. So far, the surgery has been all I chose to do. I didn't do chemotherapy or radiation. When I see the oncologist or go for my annual mammogram, there are whatever feelings are there. This is the mystery having a human experience, and everything is OK, and everything is present. There is anxiety at times waiting for results of tests. But the freedom is in not wanting the anxiety to be different.

Things started to fall apart when you met Adyashanti. What about now?

I wouldn't call it falling apart now because what seems to have happened is this mystery doesn't refuse anything. It doesn't refuse life however life moves. Liberation is not liberation *from* life. It's a liberation to live more fully.

When we really want the truth of our experience more than we want life to look a certain way, then the truth begins to reveal itself and to liberate more and more of itself within us. The mind that wants life to look a certain way is always resisting something.

Most people are looking for something to gain. The so-called ego, which doesn't really exist but we use it as a term of speech, is always looking for something for itself. "I want more peace. I want more happiness." It wants to gain something, and the process of awakening to our true nature and embodying that is the process of losing. It's the process of losing all the concepts we have, period, about what's truth. Not a single concept, not a single thought is ultimately true.

There's nothing we meet up against in our lifetime, no experience, no moment, no person, that isn't a portal to the truth of our nature, the mystery we can't really speak about. Everything is both an invitation to and an expression of that mystery. There's nothing that isn't That. It's all That. It's all an expression of That. This is That... [she laughs]... this microphone, this chair. Form is That. Emptiness is That. It's like a coin. You can't take the heads off from the tails. Only the mind can split it.

Let's get more ordinary. You mentioned you have two children.

I have a daughter who's married and has a beautiful son who is a toddler now. I have a son who is three years younger than my daughter. Family is a really important expression in my life of how this love loves itself in a family.

What do they think of you?

[She laughs.] You would have to ask them.

I'm just wondering when a person has this recognition how others see them afterwards.

When I was in my phase of "knowing" I am That and only That, rather than simply *being* what I am, I was trying to explain to my son about how I wasn't really his mother, how this was a role that was just functioning, playing like everything else, the One playing the role of mother or son, teacher, therapist, warrior, president or whatever. My mind was holding a "position" that everything was That before I knew it was also "This." At some point all of it fell away. You see, this truth doesn't require us to stand for something as a point of view.

I can remember when my son noticed that shift in me, and he said, "I'm so happy you can just be my Mom again." It was a very sweet moment because I had been holding myself in a position. It's only an ego that tries to maintain a position.

I think in my family life, there's an acceptance of me and a humanness about this as it shows up for life itself, shows up to do the laundry, be the grandma, one of the great roles I've been asked to play so far in my life. I love that role. It's been a great and utter delight.

Both of my children have been wonderful teachers, and my husband has been a great, great teacher. I didn't always imagine him so because he doesn't have an interest in *talking* about spirituality. He is an incredibly generous soul, very funny, and he is a very good weathervane for any moment where I may lack authenticity. I used to get really upset with him at times, "You just don't understand and if you understood, da, da, da, da, da." But as I look back now, I know he has been the perfect teacher because this truth, if it moves as anything, it moves as what's authentic.

We've been together 44 years. There's a lot of sharing, accepting. The older we've gotten and the more truth has been moving in our relationship, the more we just deeply respect how that is for each one of us. We are no longer trying to make the other person different in any way, an incredible gift for any human being not to feel like someone is trying to make you be something you aren't. It hasn't all been smooth, but there is a deep love, a sweetness, a humor to it all, and we are devoted to one another.

How is it for you to give satsang?

I think it is a big responsibility to put oneself out as a spiritual teacher because really there is nothing to teach. Truly, there is nothing to teach. All we're doing is pointing people back to their own Self. At least that's what I hope I am doing, not putting myself up as anything that you are not, or knowing anything that you don't know because it is not true. I'm aware of the tendency that people have to project onto the role called "spiritual teacher," and I want to be aware of not getting caught in the projections although they will be there.

How would you characterize the role of women teachers at this time?

I think it is going to be an expression that will be quite helpful in the embodiment process. In general, I think women have always been interested in living out anything, the embodiment of the truth, in the simple way—caring for children, caring for the dying, caring for parents. When the truth actually takes up residence in a body-mind, when God comes to live and move more consciously in each of our lives, we could say that this movement of love and acceptance of life as it is, is a very feminine thing.

It's not like it needs to be divided, feminine and masculine. That's another concept of course, but it's these open arms, the circle, the vessel in which everything is taking place. For me, it is a very feminine image, and it's dark. I say dark, not as opposed to light, but dark in the sense of the mystery.

This that we are is a mystery. We look out, we see mystery. We look in, we see mystery. I think the so-called masculine, the principle of penetrating, knowing, arriving at a conclusion about things, that sort of focused energy is a beautiful energy. It's an important energy, but it couldn't happen without the other. There couldn't be form without emptiness. One of my friends once said, "In the vastness that you are, where would you send something that you wanted to get rid of?" I love that. I use it often. That's the open arms of the mystery. It holds all of it, and it's not separate from anything. That's the beauty of the feminine in nature.

You recently attended an all women's retreat where there were several women teachers as leaders instead of just one famous teacher up front.

There was a deeply moving and quite powerful expression of truth in that particular retreat. We were all equal expressions of wisdom that's always present, not just the five women teachers who offered *satsang* but every single one. We're all awake consciousness; the whole world is that. The retreat was held in a circle, and we each offered what we had to offer. It was beautiful to witness the different flavors.

Spirituality and sexuality are often seen as separate, and there's not a lot of talk about sexuality in satsang. *But at this women's retreat, there was some conversation about sexuality.*

Quite a bit of conversation; there has been such a long lineage of separation of spirituality and sexuality, and it was wonderful to have that invited into the circle, women's sexuality and women's abuse. Many, many people came forward with the truth of their own experience, the parts of us as little girls that we've rejected, that may have been rejected and haven't felt welcome. So many women spoke about what has been termed the "spiritual bypass." This is where, rather than experiencing the truth of a moment of pain, confusion, etc., we move away from experience to the picture of our ideal. We move away from what's here to try to transcend it. There's a beautiful time and place to do that because we never learn what's on the other side of pain unless we have tasted the transcendence.

On the other hand, in the embodiment process, that's no longer what we are trying to do. We are actually involved, intimately involved, in meeting our moment to moment experience from non-division of our true nature. That means meeting the disowned parts of our bodies, emotions, and whatever else has been rejected. For many women, that's been sexuality. So to have your own gender and your own sexual organs be seen as your sacred space, honored, allowing that to wake up, too, not thinking that being awake means we can't be sexual.

One last thing, it seems this experience of recognition is more accessible. It doesn't seem to be only for the few.

Right, realizing who you are is available to anyone. I don't think that means that the truth is more accessible. I think that it is moving differently, but I do sense what you are speaking about. More and more people, at least in the area in which I live and work, are having beautiful, profound openings to their true nature. It's no longer the domain only of the guru or of the person we don't know from India. It is now here in our culture, in our experience, in our everyday lives.

Is having a teacher necessary?

A teacher may not be necessary in all cases, but one will appear if one is needed, and I think it's an incredible gift and blessing when that happens. In Ramana's case, the teacher was a mountain, Arunachala. Most people are looking outside of themselves and spend years, if not lifetimes, avoiding looking within. The truth has never been anywhere but in the heart of whatever the moment is, whoever we are, wherever we stand. So the invitation to look inside is ultimately what a true teacher is pointing to anyway.

There are living beings on the planet, they're grandmas, the guy at the corner store, a nurse, many, many people who are moving from a deeply awakened place who aren't being called spiritual teachers, and yet they are. Actually, everything and everyone is a teacher. The question is what are we teaching by our living?

ഇൗരൂ

After I turned off the tape, Dorothy challenged me to claim my own awareness of *That*, the mystery. We sat deep in the stillness, gazing into each other's eyes for a long while. She asked me about my own journey of awakening. I said I keep feeling I am somehow not there, and she suggested that was the mind making it up. "But I haven't experienced any bliss, union, a realization of oneness the way you and others have described it." With gentle firmness she asked, "What is here now? The formless is right here behind the eyes."

"Yes," I said. "I do have an experience of that. But I am attached to my separate self, to the 'me' story. It's really more of a habit," I said. "It's just a familiar way of constructing reality."

We walked to her car, and she gave me a book of her poetry from the trunk. I thanked her, we said goodbye, and I walked a few more blocks to where I had parked. I drove out of the city asking, "Who is seeing this view?" "Who is driving this truck?" In a couple of hours, I found a quiet spot just off Highway 1 where I could park for the night. It was soothing to hear the pounding of the surf. After dinner, I wrote by candlelight.

Dear Ulli,

Do you ever feel afraid that you are going to lose something if you surrender, if this awakeness takes over? The way Dorothy describes it, "Love comes back for itself." It doesn't sound so bad, I guess. What exactly is it that I am afraid of giving up? Talking to these women helps me see that there is really nothing to give up. Dorothy has a normal life, a husband, her kids, her work. It's not like she had to shave her head and join a monastery. No, it's not giving up anything in particular. I know what it is. It's about giving up control, even if it's just the illusion of control. It's the will to control. I want to be in charge. That is the core of it.

Suddenly a car drove up, the headlights shining onto the back of the camper. When someone knocked on the door, I knew it was probably the law. I opened the door, and there was a woman in uniform telling me that it was illegal to camp here. I said something about being from Colorado and how California has different rules. "I suppose you got too tired to continue onto Santa Cruz." I nodded. "Well, you're not bothering anyone tonight. It's OK if you want to stay." I thanked her and was glad I didn't have to find another place in the dark. I returned to my writing, describing the incident to Ulli:

I wasn't scared when I heard the car, just curious. It reminds me of what Dorothy said about the curiosity she felt even at the moment she was getting ready for surgery. Maybe that's what it's all about, just being open and curious.

Like a baby who is fascinated for no particular reason with all of the sensations and images and sounds of life. That innocence is our essential nature. No big theories, concepts, nothing to figure out. Such simplicity. I am here to experience and savor all of life. But it's not the little me. Like Dorothy said, this mystery wants a human experience, all of it. So maybe life is just about living it.

Speaking of which, I want to go outside and watch the Pacific Ocean rolling in. It is an amazing thing to be on the edge of a continent where the sea meets the land. It's all pretty amazing, actually, that there is such a thing as the sea, the land, a planet. Out of the great nothingness comes this world of form. I recently read Robert Adams describing how the world has been here for millions of years before; it will be here millions of years later. Why not relax and enjoy yourself. That puts things in perspective!

Marlies Cocheret de la Morinière

Marlies was born in Amsterdam in 1959. Now living in Santa Cruz, California, she offers *satsang* for both women and co-ed groups. She also teaches sexual healing women's retreats. Marlies is trained as a psychologist/counselor and in Hakomi, body-centered psychotherapy.

CHAPTER 6

MARLIES COCHERET DE LA MORINIERE

That's my passion, to shake everybody's booty,
to wake you up! Especially women.
Women need to take their seat.
They need to come into their power
or else nothing is going to change here.

I woke up early the next day, enjoying the solitude of the beach in the morning. The seal lying in the sand was also enjoying the quiet until I got too close to it. It jumped up and awkwardly pulled itself across the beach into the safety of the ocean.

I drove down Highway 1 to Santa Cruz in the fog. It was the first of November, the turning point between fall and winter. Santa Cruz was very quiet. Their famous boardwalk was deserted except for the seagulls and a janitorial crew. I parked the camper on a street of single-storey houses one block from the ocean. Marlies had a sign in the front asking people to use the backdoor.

I came out of the cool dampness and into a warm, bright, old-fashioned kitchen, clearly the center of the house. She served me ginger tea in a ceramic teapot and lit a candle. On the table where I set up the recorder were lemons and persimmons from her garden. There were photos on the fridge; a big one of Adyashanti, another of Ramana Maharshi. It seemed appropriate that their photos should be sitting side by side on Marlies' fridge—same lamp, different lampshade.

I remembered how I "randomly" came across Ramana's photo when I moved to Santa Fe. I was looking at a house to rent, and there was an altar with the photo placed on it. I had no idea who it was, but there was something about his look that spoke to me. Then I saw Ramana's picture on the desk of the volunteer director of the Hospice program. The third time was when I went to Pamela's *satsang*. Now I see his photo everywhere.

Marlies had a reputation for her openness, especially when it came to sexuality. At the recent retreat, sexuality was a big topic of conversation, and Marlies was not shy about it. I was looking forward to learning how she integrated sexuality and *satsang*.

∞⎰⎱

What do you remember about your early years?

In a spiritual sense, I was always on a search for something. I didn't quite know what. Now you might say I was on a search for God. There was a sense that something wasn't right. I grew up in a family where there was no religion at all. My father was Jewish but not a practicing Jew; my mother, nothing. So I went to Sunday school, and I went to different churches.

As a young girl, I was very interested in boys, not so much actively but in a funny way, I often had boyfriends. There was something very natural about that. And I was also puzzled about it. I was exploring when I was 12/13 years old with my brother. He had a girlfriend, I had a boyfriend, and we were exploring, the four of us. I felt very safe because my brother was there. Then when I was 14 or 15, I was raped. That was my real first sexual experience. Something strong changed then. There were two other times I was raped later, when I was 19 and 21. Something died, my innocence died, a sense of numbness happened. I couldn't talk about it. I didn't tell anyone.

Then many people in my life died. My parents died, the two aunts we lived with died. Every year someone died. It was discovered that I had the same illness my mother died of. Everything was right in my face so it was very hard, and at the same time, it was also an incredible gift. I wanted to be free of this. I didn't think in those words. It was more like "I want to be happy." And I knew I was unhappy.

I was an athlete. I played field hockey on the national team and that kept me alive. It kept me in my body. When I was 24, I lay sick in bed. It was all too much. I had a slipped disc. I couldn't do it anymore. I couldn't walk anymore. I think I was just burned out. I lay for two months in bed, and it was just fantastic. I had to lie down, I couldn't do anything else, my friends were taking care of me. In a funny way, it was heaven. Now I had permission to rest. I think something happened there that came together. I got my first book from Rajneesh [Bhagwan Shree Rajneesh] and thought, "This is what I want. This is it."

Two years later I was in Amsterdam biking and asked myself, "Where am I going? I am going to India." I called my brother who said, "Are you serious? When do you want to go?" I answered, "As soon as possible." My brother arranged the ticket, and I was gone in a week. I sold most of my stuff, rented out my house, everything was flowing. When I was on the plane, I wondered what the heck I was doing.

I remember arriving by bus from Bombay at the ashram in Pune where Bhagwan went after leaving Oregon. I had felt such a sigh when I sat in my first darshan even though the time with Bhagwan was difficult for me because everything opened up.

When I went to Rajneesh, I did a lot of sexual healing and meditation groups. I realized for the first time what had happened and spoke about it. It was the beginning of my journey of healing. About five years ago, the innocence started to return. I think I teach a lot about death, sex, and love because it's my own experience. I can only speak from my own experience. I cannot speak from books or anything else.

How long were you there?

I was there a year. Osho had just come back from Oregon. When I came to Pune there were only 50 people because a lot of people didn't want to be with him anymore.

So how was that being with him?

He talked about meditation in ten billion different ways and he talked a lot about tantra. When I came, there were darshans in the morning and the evening for two to three hours. He would talk about books, explain them, give his thoughts about them. I was very taken by him. It was different because he was the guru, different than my teacher right now, Adyashanti. It was very different.

Is it because he wanted to be on that guru pedestal or was it his followers who put him there?

I think it was both. I remember him speaking on one of his last birthdays, and he said he was absolutely content and was just radiant. He said, "You will experience this someday, maybe today, maybe tomorrow." Everybody went, "Yah, yah," and everyone kind of laughed. He was saying that, but we did not quite believe him because it felt like he was up there, and we were down here. It was not so much that he didn't give that message. I know for myself I was projecting that. One day I might be enlightened, I thought, but not for a few more lifetimes.

So after Pune did you move back to Amsterdam?

Yes, I went back and forth to India a few times. I was studying psychology. In the middle of my studies, I went to India. I finished my degree when I came back and went to live in a commune for awhile. I felt the commune was not it; there was an "in" group and an "out" group. I think I was the only one studying and doing something outside of the commune, most people were working inside. Even though it was very beautiful living in the commune, it was also limited.

Rajneesh opened me up to go "out." It was basically love, sex, and rock and roll [she laughs]—and lots of meditation. Just after Rajneesh, I met Barry Long. My experience with him was very much "in," very structured and bringing all that expressiveness inward, into a container.

With Adya, it feels like the whole container dropped away and just emptied out.

Barry Long is an Australian teacher who taught about the love between men and women. He used to come to England, Holland, and Germany. He was very straightforward, teaching woman not to doubt herself, to be herself. He taught men to honor women—not to go for sex but to go for love, bringing wakefulness into lovemaking with your partner.

In this process did you have relationships to practice this?

Yes, there were periods of aloneness then periods of three or four boyfriends at the same time. I was really exploring, sincerely exploring. I often didn't understand why men sometimes wouldn't be that present—not that I was always present. I wondered what the point was, to be with someone.

What were you looking for in relationship?

I was looking for the real thing. I did tantra training for two years where you meet every two months for six days and really explore on many levels about connecting and sexuality. I had a partner who was great because neither one of us wanted to be in relationship with each other, but at the same time we could explore fully with each other.

So here, you are having an intimate, sexual connection but no other relationship?

It was very different then, and it was absolutely right at the time. I feel connected with original Tantric Buddhism and Kashmiri Tantra that is coming more and more to life in me, like an original consort.

Tell me more about Tantric Buddhism.

It is about men going to women for teachings and only being able to receive the teachings when they honor woman, not so much the person but Woman—and the enlightenment in them that they live.

There was a period in seventh or eighth century in India when a lot of the monks came in contact with women living and singing their own expression of enlightenment. Many women were in their power, absolutely in their power. Tantra doesn't equal sex. I want to make that really clear. You could call that Neo-Western tantra. Tantra is a whole way of living this life, basically saying yes to all that is. It includes everything... the direct path, knowing you are *That* and bringing it forth.

It's also called the secret teachings of Buddha because Buddha didn't talk much about That. The real relationships were hardly talked about because a lot of people weren't capable of thinking that way, where men and women are seen as absolutely equal.

Back to your story... somehow you got to America.

Yes, when I was with Barry in Australia I met a guy there, Tim, from Santa Cruz. A year later, I saw him again in Boulder when I was attending Barry's workshop. We met at the lobby of the hotel, we were both single and we said, "OK, let's see how it is." We had a very nice time. He asked me if I would visit him in Santa Cruz and I said, "I am never going to live in America. This country is sick." Later I was visiting my sister who lived in Chicago, and I thought about going to Santa Cruz just to visit. I called Tim and said, "I'll come."

I went and really enjoyed it. I wasn't sure I wanted to live in Santa Cruz. But when I got back to Amsterdam, I was biking and thought, "Yeah, what do I have to lose?" I returned 11 years ago and was with Tim for a year. Then I met my husband, Joseph, also called Mokshananda.

How did you meet him?

We met in an African dance class. I didn't want to be with any man. Joe wanted to ask me out, and my girlfriend said to him, "Marlies has no interest in any man." I remember walking down the street just looking at the floor thinking, "I don't want to see anybody. Forget it." One day he asked me if I wanted to go to the movies, and I said, "OK." Since then we've been together. It was like a soft wind.

Do you share the same path?

He is strongly connected to Gurumayi who he had his awakenings with. Joe introduced me to Gurumayi, and I introduced Joe to Advaita. I met Gangaji in Holland 12 years ago when she had her first *satsang* in Amsterdam, a tiny little group.

Did you get it with Gangaji?

The first time, not really, but when I was in America, I started going to Gangaji again first with Tim, then with Joe. I took Joe to see Isaac Shapiro, an Advaita teacher. That was really big for Joe, and we shared that together. Seven years ago, a friend of ours told us about Adyashanti. When we went there, that was it.

What is it about Adya that you knew "this was it"?

[She pauses.] I knew when I met him and sat with him that this was it. I just felt a recognition. I know I have a bunch of past lives with Zen. I don't know how I know, but I know. I used to be Adya's cook at a lot of the retreats, and I became closely connected to him.

With Gurumayi I feel this blazing radiance. She's like bliss-of-being-walking. You can feel she's coming a mile away. She does *satsang* with twenty thousand people. What I enjoy so much with Adya is that I can call him up and say, "How ya doing? What's going on?" It's very ordinary. In a way, Gurumayi is like Bhagwan, not very approachable for me.

You used the word "awakenings" as if it is a multiple kind of experience.

I can't remember any one particular moment in time. One morning I was having breakfast with one of my girlfriends and she said, "Something has really changed with you." I acknowledged that. She said, "I am really happy for you." "Yeah, I'm happy for me, too." That was it. [She laughs.] I feel I just slipped in. In a way, I'm kind of a dry person. I don't have many spiritual experiences, no big highs, no blissed-out feelings. From my experience, it has mostly been silence. That's my experience of awakening. Feel silence, see silence, be silence, eternal silence. I have no idea how it happened.

I like hearing that. A lot of us think that it's got to be a particularly big ah-ha moment.

Yeah, that's only when a book is interesting, when it's this big supersonic awakening which is true for a lot of people but not for me. For me, it was going to the different teachers, doing a lot of therapy, and this sense of being emptied out. It was one step at a time.

How do you know that there's a difference from how you were before?

It just is, I don't know how else to say that. It just is. Everything flows in through the front and goes out through the back. It doesn't stick anymore.

You said there was a time when you wanted to be happy. How did that evolve?

I went from a time of being in unconscious hell to conscious hell to conscious heaven. I'm not very much touched by what happens. At the same time, I am deeply touched by what happens. Adya talks about a fringe benefit of awakening; it just starts flowing. That's been my experience. I experience absolute trust in what is. I experience silence in the midst of any kind of turmoil.

At this period in my life, a lot of things have changed because my husband and I are going to separate, but that process has been so beautiful. He is present. I am present, staying in the truth every day with what wants to happen, what wants to move naturally. In the process, I notice there is sadness, there is anger, and there is happiness—everything under the sun. At the same time, there is deep relaxation. That tells me something is very different.

It's interesting to hear how you are separating, bringing in a quality of awareness.

It's very conscious. We want to feel all the emotions and not blame each other. We did a closing ritual together, honoring each other and thanking each other for the time together. It was really sweet. We don't know if we want to get divorced or not. We just know that at this point, we need to separate. He needs to do what he needs to do. I need to do what I need to do.

Why are you certain that you need to separate?

There is a desire to take a deeper seat in myself. When I went with a bunch of girlfriends to Tassajara a few months ago, it got really clear. I wanted to be met more deeply. I knew something more was possible, that there was something not happening here. Then the process started.

Two months later, my husband met another woman. That really pushed the envelope. I suggested, "How about if you don't have contact with her for a month, we sit together, and we see what really wants to happen here between us?" One day we woke up and he asked me, "How are you doing?" I told him, "I'm doing well. I think it's clear to me. We need to separate." He said, "I feel exactly the same." We looked at each other, and we started laughing. "OK, I guess this is it then."

I feel the sadness, and I also feel so much excitement. Something is coming to life. When I was teaching last week in the women's retreat, I could feel everything had come together. You know how you sometimes do something that you have done for a long time, but it feels like the first time? That's what it felt like.

Is jealousy present?

No, just sadness. We were together for nine years. When he was connecting with her, I could feel anxiety, but in a funny way, I also felt a deep love for this woman. I actually called her. She sounds like a very lovely person. It was painful, but I never felt jealousy.

I can see there's something important happening for my husband and something important is happening for me. I am taking more of a seat in myself, and I can see that in my husband as well. There is a tremendous gift here. We are both clear that the relationship as it is needs to die. Either we come together and it will be new, or we won't come together, and we will have a divorce.

Do you have children?

No. I have a kidney disease. That's what my mother died of. We tried to get pregnant, and I did get pregnant, but I had a miscarriage. I was really relieved because I was so extremely tired. I remember talking with my doctor about it, Joe was with me and I asked, "Do you think it's a good idea to get pregnant?" The doctor said, "No. You will survive, but it will take a tremendous toll on your body. You will be very tired." We looked into adoption, but it just didn't feel right.

In the satsang *focused on relationship, what do you share?*

We talk about how relationship is different when there is wakefulness, the awareness that there is just One. We talk about honesty, attraction, the plain day-to-day things. People come in and ask questions not only about their love relationships but any kind of relationship. I find that a lot of people spiritualize everything away into emptiness. I have no interest in that. I talk a lot about ordinary stuff, what happened that day and maybe a teaching about it.

For relationship *satsang* or any kind of *satsang*, I just ask myself, "What wants to be spoken?" At the recent woman's retreat I said, "I want to talk about women, sex, and love. Are you ready?" A lot of women, one out of three, if not one out of two, have been sexually abused. You wake up, and you have this emptiness that's being experienced here in the chest. The heart opens, and it's really warm and loving, but it's cut off. What happens down here? [She gestures below her waist.] Then they start spiritualizing everything away. I don't want to be a teacher who talks about truth only in the sense of emptiness.

What about your own healing around sexual abuse?

I did a lot of therapy, but what really changed it, besides waking up, is that I did a lot of hands-on sexual healing with women. First my teacher taught me, and then I shared it with other women. I still do. It's about going internally to the sacred spot, the "g" spot and massaging it because it wants to wake up. Women have unlimited potential, *unlimited*. The sacred spot holds all the pleasure and all the pain. When you start massaging a woman there, often it's numb, dead. Then rage, pain, burning—everything can come. And pleasure. That really opened up a lot for me energetically—not only vaginal orgasms but also a sense of pleasure in my yoni.

This is a time when women need to take their seat. This is the root, the first and second chakra, our ground. We need to come into our power or else nothing is going to change here.

So when you say take your seat, you mean it literally.

Exactly, so that's what I talk about, how important it is not to cut ourselves off, and just be in the heart, and la-la-la which is fine, but it's not very connected. At the retreat there were a lot of women who said, "I didn't know you could talk about sexuality at *satsang*. We always just talk about awakeness." There was a lot of relief. At the beginning I said, "I'm here to shake everybody's booty." A lot of women came up to me afterwards and told me that I had done just that. Many women started sharing about their sexual abuse and how they didn't talk about it in *satsang* because you're not supposed to. A lot of "supposed to's" were killed.

How do you think it is different talking about it in satsang *versus talking about it with a therapist?*

A lot of therapists are not awake. They're just trying to change the personality or make you feel better. That has its function, and it's very beautiful. In *satsang*, it's truth. That brings wakefulness to whatever is talked about. If it's about sex or whatever, it doesn't really matter. What is often forgotten is that *everything* is included in *satsang*. People think it's OK to talk about emptiness, silence, and yeah, a little bit of emotion but not too much. It's not OK to talk about anything that's not spiritual. But to me, everything is spiritual.

Tell me about the statue you recently bought.

When I saw the statue, Kuan Yin, I was so taken by it. She's standing on a really big dragon, and I realized that is exactly what needs to happen for me. It represented standing absolutely in my power, in my Self. In the *satsang* and my daily life, I can feel more and more that I'm just myself, but I still feel there is not an absolute fullness. I want it all the way.

What is it about the image of standing on the dragon that seems to relate to women's power?

It's standing on your own two feet. So many women are dependent on someone else and don't really dare to live the truth. Men, too, but I'm a woman so I can talk about that. Women need to stand up. That's my opinion. That's my opinionated opinion. [She laughs.]

What will happen if that happens, women standing on their own two feet?

Well, just look at the world. It's very patriarchal. A lot of women are married to these patriarchal guys who are supporting them. I understand they love their men, but I am curious about how much they are really living in their truth or are just afraid to stand on their own two feet.

Hilary Hart writes in her book about a Jesuit monk who is asked, "What could change this world?" He replies, "When women come into their power." When I read it, I said, "Yes, that's exactly it." That's my passion; my passion is to shake everybody's booty. My wish is for everybody to wake up, especially women. It doesn't matter if you're a man or a woman. Awake is awake. It has nothing to do with gender.

How do you see relationship now?

I don't see relationship as a chance for healing although for a long time, I saw it that way. I don't have any interest in that anymore. It's healed. It's done. There's nothing to heal anymore.

It's absolutely impersonal. It's just here. Love. It's being here, absolutely here with whatever is or whatever is not. You have a choice.

Where do you want to reside, in your head or your heart? Going with the flow, going with what is.

Another thing I would like to explore is what you are seeing in the way people are waking up right now.

I see many different things. I see people who just wake up at the drop of a hat. I see people who struggle and struggle and struggle, and everything in between.

What is going on when there is so much struggle?

A part of the struggle is not wanting to be here, not wanting to face what needs to be faced, and constantly wanting to go out there instead of going in here and saying, "Gee, I'm really struggling. Let's get curious about that. What is that about?"

I notice a lot of people are at first very afraid. You can see that as a therapist also. Then something turns, a sense of sinking in, and they get curious. Let's experience everything as it is. Let's go in there.

That sounds like Hakomi work. Do you use Hakomi often?

Yes, a lot, but it's all about letting go of everything that you think you are supposed to be. If it's a Hakomi therapist or a *satsang* teacher, all the beliefs that come with that, you let it go. Now it's just about being myself which is so wonderful.

What do you think you're offering just by your presence that's unique?

The feedback I often hear is that others feel free to talk about anything. I don't think there's anything that puts me off, really. In a lot of ways, I am very direct. I don't spiritualize things; I just name it as it is. I'm kinda simple; I'm not someone who tells long stories. I live in the not-knowing until I know. I also say enjoy yourself, have a good time. I say it because in my own experience, I felt so much heaviness and so much seriousness.

Is there anything else you want to share?

Awakeness is always here. When I first heard that I knew it between my ears. Now I can say, really, it has always been here. It was here when I was a little girl. It was here before I was even here. It is so obvious now, and it is so funny that I didn't know that.

During the process with my husband, I met myself. I met me or I met "I." I don't know how else to express that. I don't need anyone or anything to meet me from the outside anymore. Everything is met within and without. I am absolutely content, just what I wished for one day after I heard Osho mention that. What a relief. It is done. What a blessed life!

I also find that the biggest teacher is life itself because that's when the rubber hits the road as my teacher told me. I am very grateful for all the teachers and sages of all times, very grateful for this life, very grateful for what is given and taken away, so precious, this life.

ഗ

After leaving Marlies' cozy kitchen, I headed out into the dark night looking for the campground where I could park the camper. I took the wrong exit off the freeway and got lost. It was a great relief when I finally got settled, fed the dog, had some dinner, and then sat down to continue my letter:

Dear Ulli,
It's so interesting talking to all these women about their relationships. Everyone has such a different story which helps keeping me from getting stuck, thinking that it has to look a certain way. First there's Pamela

who is single. At least for now. And there's Marlies who was married to a spiritual teacher, but now it looks like they are separating. Chameli is also with a teacher, and they have created a practice out of their relationship. Sharon's husband isn't a teacher, but he definitely shares the same path.

Then there's Dorothy and Muni. Here are two women who are fully awake and happily married to men who don't participate in that way in their lives. I am especially touched by their complete acceptance of their partners and their unique gifts. There's no judgment, no expectations.

After we turned off the tape recorder, Marlies asked me, "What keeps you from knowing that you are awake?" "I don't really know," I said. "The answer that automatically comes up doesn't work anymore. I haven't had the big bang wake-up experience. But you didn't either."

I have been thinking about Marlies' reaction when Osho said something about "One day you will feel this peace, this contentment." She thought, "Sure. Someday but not for a few more lifetimes." But it wasn't a few more lifetimes, it was just a few more years. It makes me think that this enlightenment business is not so far off. For anyone.

All I know is that I love being around these women. It's the resonance that Sharon talked about. When awake consciousness talks to sleeping consciousness, the sleeping consciousness is more likely to make the leap of awakening.

Maybe that's the only thing we can actually "do" on this path. We put ourselves in places where we can be exposed to others who are living their life from this awake place. And the rest is grace.

Karen McPhee

Karen was born in 1962 in Nova Scotia. For the past five years, Karen has been inspiring a growing number of people with her teachings of *The Power of Now* and sharing the essence and wisdom of her personal experience of living the awakened life. Karen lives in Calgary where she shares her current message of fully claiming one's inner teacher and relying on the truth and wisdom within.

CHAPTER 7

KAREN MCPHEE

All the aspects of our human nature
are not only welcomed, but celebrated.
It's enough of "just surviving,"
it's time to dance!

I returned from California in the middle of November. Without a second thought, or any thoughts really, I knew it was time to move back to Colorado. It was clear that my chapter in Santa Fe was complete. I had gone there to discover the direct path, and I was immensely grateful for that. But now I realized that I didn't need to go away to find what was already here. Within two weeks I packed up my personal belongings in Santa Fe and returned to the mountains, to my community, to Chris.

Chris wasn't surprised. He always knew I would come home. "You're a Colorado girl. You belong here," is how he put it. At the time I thought he was in denial about my moving to Santa Fe, but when I returned, I realized that he was probably right. I do belong in these mountains, on this mesa. I had to admire his patience with me. Yes, he missed me and said so many times, but he never got dramatic about the situation, making some kind of ultimatum about how I better come home or else.

The first thing we did when I moved back was install a wood stove. I wanted a cozy nest to spend the winter. At nine thousand feet in elevation, it's the real thing. The snow is deep, and sometimes we can't drive in or out. We spend a lot of energy on keeping the fire going, shoveling snow, getting the truck unstuck.

The days grew shorter, and I stopped working on the book. Winter is a natural time to slow down, so that's what I did. I skied, I worked, I read. I made Christmas cards and wrote a poem for the winter solstice:

Just as the earth
Leans away from the sun
I welcome the darkness
Knowing it's all One

Poised on the edge of the
Great Mystery
I embrace the void
Formless and free

May you be at peace
In the stillness of night
Knowing the gifts of both
Darkness and light.

As the days gradually grew longer, I began to feel the pull to continue writing. I had hoped to meet Karen again in person to do the interview, but she had recently had a car accident and wasn't offering workshops in the States anymore. I couldn't afford to travel to Canada, so I scheduled a phone appointment instead. Before I dialed her number, I made myself a cup of tea and curled up in the big overstuffed chair in my bedroom where I could look out the windows at the quiet, white landscape.

Karen started our interview with a couple of minutes of silence. She invited me to relax into the here and now, letting the breath take us to formlessness. Her voice was hypnotic. Because she is intimate with stillness, it has always been easy to go there with her. Silence outside, silence inside. I felt full like I had just had a satisfying meal. "It's so simple," I said. "So simple," she sighed.

ॐ

I really enjoy the story, even though I know it's not about the story. In your life, what stands out in your memory that was different from other people?

When I was very young, probably not even five, there was an awareness present that didn't seem to be necessarily present in everyone around me. I would know if someone was standing behind me, who it was, and what mood they were in even if I couldn't tell from my other senses. My mother said I was always calm and quiet and just inside myself.

When you said, "What stands out as being different," the next major thing that flashed is that I had thyroid cancer when I was 16. You are somewhat removed from normal social interaction when you have cancer, especially at that age. People don't know how to be with that. No one is totally mature yet. There was one other person in high school who had a different form of cancer than I did, and he died. I know that separated me, not just from other people, but from a standard ordinary life where you get married and have children. Still to this day, I can look back and know that was a turning point. You face your own mortality.

It sounds like you didn't follow the more traditional path of growing up, getting married, and having children.

No! I tried to. [She laughs.] There were relationships and stuff, but it just never would fall into place. Most of my relationships up until my late 20s didn't last for any length of time. I did have that sort of program running, "Yeah, I'm going to get married and have kids." It still seemed like that was the thought of what the life was going to be like, but there was just never any evidence to support it.

So what instead was happening?

An awful lot of suffering. I experienced a violation at a critical age of development that I don't want to go into detail about. A bad character came along one summer when I was about 13, and the violations I experienced through having cancer were very intense for a young woman of that age. "Gee, we'd like to bring our 12 young male interns and come in to look at your tumor... do you mind?" Then they take all your clothes off. Because of the nature of the personality that I was given, there was too much shyness to stand up and say, "No, you can't," and my mother wasn't there at the time or else she would have kicked their butts.

The reason I bring it up is because it's been fairly clear that all those things that happened brought up this state of inner self-hatred, lack of worthiness. Everyone has it to some degree. It's just that it was quite intense for me. From the time I was nine years old, I wanted to die. So something just wasn't right. Then you add the violation and the cancer. From that time on, it was 24 hours a day agony, internal self-hatred, and it was just awful. I really felt like I didn't belong here, didn't deserve to be alive here or something.

Did you ever try to commit suicide?

Let's just say I seriously contemplated it. Through the 20s, there was a lot of self-abuse, depression, drug and alcohol abuse. Then in my late 20s, something happened. I went into therapy, and that's when awareness started to wake up. One of the milestones of that period was the end of a relationship. There were no relationships at all. I couldn't have gotten a date if I'd paid for one. Nothing was happening in my life.

It was a coming to terms with what was going on inside me without numbing myself with alcohol, drugs, sex, or anything. I got in touch with the depth of suffering, self-hatred and all that stuff. It was about a three-year period. For most of that, I was in a black depression, and the last year of it I wanted to end it all. So yes, I definitely got to a dark place.

During those three years, what did your life look like? Did you go to work?

Did you have friends?

I was still operating a semi-normal life. I was working in the computer industry, so I had a fairly solid career but outside of work, not much going on. I separated from my family and didn't see them much because it became clear to me that I didn't know who I was, and I didn't want someone repeating the story of who I was. I wanted to find out for real, for myself. I think it was challenging for my family, especially my twin sister. I was finally experiencing the emotions that had been repressed my whole life. It was very deep grieving, and I needed to have space to deal with it, so I had to withdraw.

Is there anything about having a twin sister that made your life unique?

The only way I can answer that is that some of the deepest work I did in the early years had a lot to do with the issues that twins face. Sometimes twins have an intense need for either space or intimacy. There's no question I went the way of needing space because of never having any. From the moment I was born, there was someone beside me, either in the crib or the twin bed next to me, up until I was out of the house at about 17. This was a really big deal all those years ago. When I started to go inward, it was tough for my twin because I think she felt like she was losing the other half of herself, and that increased my need for space.

Any support in this process?

By that time, I had gotten in touch with meditation. You know, a lot of us start with this New Age stuff, positive thinking. I was in that phase. I had begun to explore some spiritual groups, meditation groups, chanting groups. I began to hook up with some people who were as weird and as dysfunctional as I was, which you often find on the spiritual path. [She laughs.]

You said something about how after the three years, it shifted.

Yeah, there was inner exploration, books I was reading, and some people who came into my life. Around that time a man, a partner, came into my life.

The very first sort of recognition I really remember is when I was watching Deepak Chopra, and he said simply, "Become aware of the one who is watching." To my knowledge, that was the beginning of the spontaneous "whatevers" that happened over the years. I wasn't on a path, not that I knew of.

I would just keep having these experiences of reality opening up. Once I was in the backseat of the car, and I looked over to the people in the car beside me and saw utterly through the illusion of separation. But what I also saw was how separation is created and sustained, even though it's an illusion. It was shocking. The people in the car next to me were pretending they didn't know I was there. They were in this illusion that they didn't know we were One. I was not in that illusion in that moment, and it was excruciatingly painful.

Around the same time, a really major thing happened. The man who came into my life for many years showed me a videotape of the man who catalyzed his awakening. This man was a teacher for awhile. He was radically alive, and then he disappeared.

What happened when you watched the videotape?

Because of everything that had gone before, there was a readiness here, and the transmission of truth from this man was so potent. It was the first time I had been exposed so directly. Through video, it's virtually the same as being there. I was completely open. My partner didn't even tell me it was a spiritual teacher. I was so overwhelmed that we didn't even get to the end of the tape. I just walked outside and laid on the front step. I couldn't move.

It sounds like there was a series of openings for you.

Yes. It was practically a daily experience that all this stuff was happening to me for a number of years.

Was there any one particular moment that felt like there was no turning back?

The one that is probably of the most interest is the day I first met Eckhart Tolle. That was the day. I had found my way to *The Power of Now* in the most delicious way as most people do. I was beginning to withdraw more and more from the world, living primarily in stillness except for a part-time job and the minimum I had to do to keep my relationship afloat. So most of the time I was sitting on park benches by the river. No one knows I am doing this, right? My partner is going to work all day, and after work I am going to sit in the park.

A friend of my partner comes over and says, "Hey, there's this new spiritual teacher." By this time I am out of the closet, we're all going to gatherings and reading books, and we had been sitting with another teacher. He says, "This guy spent two years on a park bench," and my whole world stopped moving. Everything stopped. He pulled the book out of his knapsack, handed it to me, I put my hand on the book and said, "I'm sorry. I have to go." I just left and went to the bookstore. I came home, sat under my apple tree for the next two weeks, and did nothing else, maybe get up, get something to eat, maybe teach a class, and then I was back under the tree with the book.

You were under your bodhi tree.

Yeah, you bet. I still miss that tree. At that point, *The Power of Now* had sold only a few copies. The book had just come out. I inquired about bringing Eckhart to Calgary, and a long story short, things got worked out.

We arranged a luncheon with Eckhart and another teacher we were sitting with. I also arranged for Eckhart to come to our home to give a small *satsang* that night for six of my closest friends. Can you imagine! I'm reluctant to confess that because now it's unimaginable to have such a small intimate gathering with Eckhart.

We go to the luncheon, I have not met Eckhart yet, and he has not met me. We're at the cafeteria, I'm outside on the sidewalk looking around, and I see this man walking towards me. I'd seen the picture from the book cover and I thought, "Gee, that might be Eckhart." There were all kinds of people all over the place, and he walked directly to me, right up to me. He looked me in the eye [she starts to cry] and he said, "I know that you must be Karen." Gosh, I haven't talked about this for years.

I'm glad you're sharing it now.

The emotion is interesting because I am in a very different phase, and it is so lovely to go back and remember. That day was just magical. The seating arrangements were such that I was sitting directly across from both Eckhart and the other teacher, so I was getting beamed. This transmission by both of them for three hours was really juicy. I felt a resonance with Eckhart that was extraordinary. I was so aware of his every breath. It was just indescribable. Here's the neat part. When it was time to leave, we all got into my partner's car. Normally, I would sit in the front but invisible hands were on my body shoving me in the backseat, and Eckhart got in beside me.

This whole thing, I can't capture it right now, but there was this orchestration of offering him a ride, getting into the backseat. It was divine. Eckhart's associate got into the front seat with my partner, and they are in this conversation. Eckhart and I are sitting in the backseat in silence, and he silently reaches over, puts his hand on mine, and that was the moment. That was it. Suddenly, it was known to me that I am the universe. It was a number of years ago, but I can still get that sense of "ahhhh." It was the first time I had ever sat beside someone who wanted nothing from me. There was nobody there. There was no agenda. You could say it was like an invitation to rest in Self. That went on for however long the car ride was. No words, just wow, and I knew something big had happened.

It feels like there was stillness and peace around that, not something dramatic.

It was peaceful, and it was so vast, so enormous. It was like they say in Advaita, the non-experience. It was beyond any personhood. The thing of it is, though, it destroyed my life. That's how enormous it was, but subtle at that moment. [She laughs.]

Little did you know the trickery of it.

Yes, the way that the teacher woos you whether he or she knows they're doing it or not, the way that life woos you. [She laughs.] I had some private time with him that day, and again we just sat in stillness. So, I am in stillness with this man virtually all day except for about an hour or two. At the end when it was time for me to leave, he said something to me about my destiny as a teacher. That was huge. "OK, now I know my destiny. Now I know what I'm here for."

After that, I dedicated my life to the teaching a hundred per cent. I was already completely dedicated to the teaching before I even met Eckhart. I gave his book to a number of people. I then spent the next year doing nothing but spending every spare moment either speaking to Eckhart on the phone or going to one of his events. I was flying back and forth, attending everything he offered, and working with him privately. That's all I did for at least a year.

Then I moved to Vancouver into an apartment in Eckart's building that became available. That was another miracle. I moved in next to him by the unbelievable grace that opened that space for me, and I lived there for about a year.

What was happening in your relationship during this time?

My partner was instrumental in facilitating this thing with Eckhart. He said, "This is your life, your destiny. Just go, forget me." Those were not idle words. He meant it. He was behind me all the way. When I moved to Vancouver I couldn't get work. My partner supported me through part of it, and he wasn't exactly rich.

My relationship with Eckhart wasn't ever romantic, but it was extremely intimate as it is with your true teacher. When I was in Vancouver my partner and I still had a relationship, but there was no question what my priority was, and it was also his priority. The relationship was never the same again after that, but we loved each other very much, so it took quite awhile for the relationship to formally dissolve into just friendship. I don't think that one will ever be over. It just changed form.

How did you start teaching?

I moved to Vancouver in July, and I volunteered to be Eckhart's personal assistant. People would phone for private meetings or other concerns regarding Eckhart, and I would sit with them and just be in this field of stillness. I would listen, take notes. Then I would get the list, sit with Eckhart, go through each person, and Eckhart would just be in the stillness and listen for himself.

One day a woman called, and for some reason very much to my surprise, it came into my awareness that I could somehow be of service to her. I never did anything with that, didn't write it down, and later that day when I was going through the list of say ten people, I got down to her, telling Eckhart about her. As soon as I was finished, he paused and said "You can help her." There was such a synchronicity, and that's how it started. She came over for a private session.

Very shortly after that I started doing groups, and Eckhart helped get the word out. Looking back, it's really an amazing thing to have that much support from the teacher. It just happened. I don't think it was even two months after I got there.

What was it like to move into that role?

It was as natural as breathing. By then, of course, there was an awareness that it's all just presence. That's all there is. There wasn't any sense that I as a person had to do anything. I saw in that moment everything I had ever done had led me to that moment, all of these weird and wacky classes I had taken, career paths I had started down, maybe didn't finish. So it just clicked. It was like coming home.

At some point it became clear that a website was needed. We wanted to let people know where Eckhart's teaching events were and about other teachers who were going to be emerging through Eckhart's teaching. I got on the web and not long after that the book started to really take off, people started finding his website, and invitations came in for me to teach in other places.

Then I had to leave Vancouver and return to Calgary because of an illness. I went to Calgary to recuperate but got back doing events again for another couple of years.

The illness you just talked about, your car accident recently, and your cancer at age 16, you seem to have a lot of...

Karma. All I know is that I needed to leave Vancouver and return to Calgary. Once I became ill, there was no longer a choice about it. Yet I resisted until the last possible moment because I misunderstood what the role of the teacher is. There were still a lot of concepts around what Eckhart was to me, and essentially I was holding onto him in a way that was not appropriate. I thought he was "it." He was my salvation. He never encouraged that in any way. He always said to all of us, "It's in you." It was my own conditioning and projection going on.

Maybe it's the same thing with the car accident. I needed to stop traveling, and I needed to stop teaching *The Power of Now*. I knew those two things. Still I had difficulty making the transition. In any event, my car was rear-ended, and I got a bit of whiplash. It definitely put the period at the end of the sentence of everything I was in the process of closing.

There are things that have happened as a result of this accident I could not have expected. I don't know if any of us truly knows what is going to happen next, why, for what purpose. It's more about saying yes to what happens rather than trying to figure it out. The accident has caused me to get a lot of healing and bodywork that I otherwise would not have done. Some ancient conditioning has been released in the process—so deep in the tissue.

You have said that being a teacher accelerates the embodiment process.

In my experience, yeah. Teachers use the word embodiment differently. What I know about it now is that it's not something that has a completion. It never stops. What I call embodiment is coming to terms with the world of form in a new way so it is seen for what it is: it's the formless. Quantum mechanics tells us our very bodies are made out of nothing. Consciousness is all there is.

There are great teachers, and they all have a specific destiny and purpose. I can't speak for Eckhart, but maybe in his case his role is to be the embodiment of stillness and model what it is to live in the present moment. It's essential. It's caused many people to wake up.

And there's something else going on. My experience is that just to be in love with the stillness is not enough. It's almost as if one has to be in love equally with form as the formless. Many teachers get this, maybe more so now, but there was a time when this kind of language wasn't used, at least not that I could see. All the teachings seemed to be pointing to the Absolute, and that's great, that's real, that's primary. Until you've got that, there's no point talking about embodiment. But then something else happens.

I've heard some teachings about this, and they refer to something called the "return." Apparently this is the Tantric path. The first phase is that you withdraw to some degree from normal worldly stuff and go within. You die to stillness, you die to true nature, and you hang out there as long as required. Then the Self wants to know its manifestation, to participate in the human experience *as* the Self.

I had an almost total withdrawal. I spent a number of years primarily in stillness and meditation just functioning enough to keep a life going—barely. Then all of a sudden one day this movement started to happen from within, to come back into the body, into the personality, into the world, and an intense passion started to wake up. This "return" is about becoming ever more grounded in one's true nature *and* in the world. In my experience, it is very challenging. Hanging out in stillness is the easy part.

I think it's important to know the whole circle, to know the map. Having this experience of enlightenment or awakening, that's not the goal.

Yes! That's what I see over and over again, this suffering, this struggle that comes because people think there is this destination, and they don't seem to be arriving "there." This is a common example of denying what is, resisting what is. If we have some ideal in consciousness about what it "should" be like, and this moment isn't matching it, we suffer because we resist what is actually going on. It's the comparison to an ideal that causes this angst.

So how do we get these ideals? One way is by making an image up about the spiritual teacher and comparing ourselves to the image. Often "gurus" are presented as beyond human, and I feel that is a disservice to the followers. There is no perfection on the level of the human. Even if the guru is the most pure, clear, enlightened being of all time, they are still human. *And*, we are projecting our own image onto them in any case. We don't *really* know what it is like over there where they are. We only have an image here in our mind.

The other way we get this ideal is from the peak experience, the one that comes from this moment of satori or enlightenment that we once experienced, often on a retreat. We get the idea that it's supposed to be our 24/7 permanent state if we are truly liberated. Since all states come and go, this is impossible. Yet we suffer because we compare our ordinary moments to this peak experience and tell ourselves the story that we aren't "there" yet because this moment isn't as good as that peak experience. I honestly can say I don't think I have met anyone, in all these years, who didn't suffer from this to some degree.

This is my one passion right now. If I get going on it, it's really intense. How I say it now is: the moment of the deepest recognition, whether it happens to you over a hundred moments or in one moment is just the beginning. Realizing one's true nature—that's just the beginning. Then it becomes about embodying that in one's human life and in the world. No one can do that for us.

That's what I would like to offer people. We don't know what's going to happen for sure with an individual. As Anandamayi Ma said, "If there are six billion people, then there are six billion ways to awaken."

I want to explore the way you see death now.

Years ago a book by Krishnamurti came to me, and there's a passage where he talks about death. He said that the problem is that we push death into the future, and that creates so much fear and also denial. He invited us to bring death closer, get it right here.

Quite often when I wake up in the morning, I wake up in stillness. I luxuriate in that for awhile, and then things start to come. Usually one of the first things that comes is, "Well, this person, this body, is going to die." It's just right here. One of the greatest freedoms and what has made living possible for me is to keep death as close as the breath, right here. As with everything, we can't really talk about it. It's just words, "Yeah, yeah, that sounds like a good idea," but I'm talking about an internal reality. The reality is that this body will die and keeping that sense alive. It sounds morbid, but it's not. It is *so* freeing.

Let's talk about relationships.

The first thing that comes to me is that all these things we would rather not have happen or we go through only because we have to—emotions, the painful stuff—I love that. I just *love* that. That which is considered unpleasant or what we don't want to go through, I now worship... anger, pain, loss, grief. I celebrate it.

This is a part of what we're calling embodiment. There isn't fear or reluctance to have the painful part of life. There's a relaxing into the reality that it is birth, death, up, down. Even in nature, things cycle. I'm so in love with everything that arises, whether it's a so-called good feeling or a so-called bad or challenging feeling. Anger to me is a goddess. I worship her. When she comes, it is just evidence of how great a human being can be that they could be visited by such a divine entity as anger or pain or sorrow. Oh my God. I love that stuff.

Relationship. Everything that comes is divinely orchestrated whether it's an emotion or a person or an event, whether it's a friendship or an intimate partner. I forgot whose teaching this is, but they talk about how relationship in the beginning is to help you know yourself, and that part is just awful. Whether it's many relationships or one, it's pain, it's drama and it sucks. But as the recognition of Self gets more stabilized or embodied, the relationship is there to be able to celebrate all the facets. Let's say that life is a diamond with many facets, and you're so in love with the differences, the diversity.

Eckhart says in *The Power of Now* that relationship is there to make you conscious, not to make you happy. I would say up until a point, that's really true. Then as presence emerges, relationship can be as much or more about shared joy, shared recognition, shared being. When you can interact with people from that place, especially romantic relationships which are definitely the most challenging as far as I can tell, there's a space that's created. That space is a space of love where that which is "unlove" can come in and be met. If I or my partner is going through an old pattern coming up, some huge piece of pain, that stuff is welcome. It's not just welcomed, it's invited: "Come in." Because the two beings are so clear about that. This idea, "Oh, you're doing something wrong, or you're hurting me," falls away. There's a courage that comes. No matter how ugly or painful or messy this is, it's welcome in this space. When it's healed or set free, there's more space inside each one and more love comes through. It's all good news.

We also need to see that we're all on different paths. I know so many people have such deep pain over this, and I've had more than my share over it, where you don't seem to find your partner. Yet you see other people who do, maybe even fairly early in life. They meet this one person, and they can grow together. It's so beautiful, but it's not the way for most people I've met. Not all, but most that are in this, let's say "awakening," find that our relationships tend to cycle or there will be long periods of not having a romantic partner. Coming to terms with that is very important and helpful. If you see what the true purpose of relationship is, it's easier to let people come and go as they need to.

In what way are you teaching or working now?

Well, the car accident was a gift in that it got me off the road. I've been spending a lot of time in stillness because the body can't move. What came to me, first of all, was to find a different way to deliver this message. If there's a destiny here for this person called Karen, I wouldn't want to label it "spiritual teacher" anymore because spiritual is too limiting to me. I'm interested in the whole human being. To me, it's all welcome now. It's all equal. It's all to be nourished and supported.

What does that look like?

The training I've been taking recently is more along the lines of counseling and life coaching. I happened to find an organization that is totally based in presence, but they don't call it that. You get another language which I find to be more accessible. You also get tools to assist people in living this more authentic, whole Self. I chose the organization because they call what they do "dancing in the moment" with the other person.

It feels like this is something new, instead of the old paradigm of spiritual or not spiritual. It's all the same.

That's very true. It's true in my experience, and it's true in the broader sense. Many people are sensing that a shift wants to happen. We want to have all that we are, not just welcomed but *celebrated*!!

I was doing one of these trainings, and I had this moment where I was coaching someone, and the personalities, the bodies were there interacting. I fell so in love with her. It was indescribable. I was able to fully celebrate *all* that she was—all the things about this unique person—her physical self, her personality, her quirkiness, everything. I fell in love with the form as much as I had fallen in love with formlessness. It was just one of those moments.

A lot of the spiritual teachings whether intentionally or not somehow lead to the idea that we're supposed to transcend the body, the personality. This so often leads to repression or denial. We get the message we have to work on ourselves, improve ourselves. Yet that never leads to freedom. Enough of that already!

We also get the message that we *have* to welcome or accept everything. Somehow there is the assumption that these things are "less than" or are just to be tolerated. That is actually a subtle form of resistance. All the aspects of our human nature are not only to be welcomed, but celebrated. It's enough of just surviving. It's time to dance! Everything you are is welcome.

Let's not just come to terms with it, let's see how f——g great it is!

It's almost like there's another level of waking up. We don't have the language for it yet, but there's something else, a deeper recognition about our humanness.

It seems like there's something beyond what I would have called embodiment before. It's a falling in love with it in a way I could never have expected. It is so delicious, so alive. I often say now that a human being is an art form, a magnificent creation. That's the premise I like to start with.

I've never had the experience in any *satsang* or with any teacher like what's happening to me right now. Not even close. It's a completely different realm. I'm not interested in enlightenment at all. There's a passion coming to life, a love for every unique person, and I feel it is part of this embodiment/feminine shift thing that you're writing about.

ಌಝಲ

I was inspired by the way Karen described her passion and her love for our unique humanness. It's easy for me to embrace that side, the embodiment half. But I became aware that I have missed, maybe even avoided, the first half of the process, hanging out in stillness.

A few weeks ago at Neelam's New Year retreat, I noticed how uncomfortable I was with emptiness. In a dialogue with one of the participants, Neelam asked whether it was OK to rest. The woman started crying and said, "I'm afraid to rest because I will be destroyed." I knew exactly how she felt. After talking with Karen, the same fear arose again. So I explored it further in my journal:

Karen clearly said that there needs to be a time of stillness. Many of the women say the same thing. They enjoy the silence, the emptiness. I can't relate to that. I am uncomfortable with the void. That's why I am always busy, taking care of details, never standing still. I am afraid that if the mind is quiet, if thinking stops, then that is death. Stillness is death.

It's the loss, the dissolution of the self that really scares me. I don't want to die. I know intellectually that who I am doesn't die. But on another level, there's a part of me that desperately wants to live. How else can I experience the beauty of this world? Who is going to live this life if I am no longer "me"? Ahhh, but how can I know what will happen when I let go of my grip on this separate self until I let go of my grip on this separate self? It's a kind of catch-22.

All the teachers say that the body is also consciousness. There is no "other." It's all the same. The form and the formless. Can I trust it enough to just jump out of the plane as Sharon would say? It's a leap into the unknown, a willingness to let go. What am I so afraid of?

Annette Knopp

Annette was born in 1965 in Germany. After circling the globe, she now splits her time between Costa Rica and upstate New York where she lives with her partner, Stephan, and his son, Eli. Annette hosts Circles of Presence, her term instead of *satsang*, and Women's Circles.

CHAPTER 8

ANNETTE KNOPP

The feminine principle is also about the evoking of beauty.
"She" is always present when someone decorates a house,
creates harmony or art. It is an overflow of the radiance of our
hearts and the need to bring that out.
It is the reflection that says "everything is sacred."

It was a delightful surprise when Annette and Francie called one winter morning and offered to come to Telluride to host a gathering. I knew Francie from Pamela's circle, and I had heard of Annette. She was the third member of the trio with Neelam and Pamela who sometimes offered *satsang* at the Omega Institute. Giving *satsang* as a team is evolving as part of the feminine way, and so is sitting in a circle, another reminder that there is no real difference between the "student" and the "teacher."

At the day-long event at my house, Annette spoke directly, "There is no such thing as awake or not awake." Annette was leaning forward trying to soothe Ulli who was determined to "get" it. Her suffering was obvious as tears rolled down her cheeks, and she cried, "I see it in your eyes, and I want what you have." Everyone who knows Ulli knows that she already has it! She is a loving, sweet, kind person. It's funny how we are always looking outside of ourselves for what is so obviously within us.

I do the same thing. I felt that same overwhelming feeling flood through me when sitting with Neelam a few weeks before. I started crying, "I just want to gaze into the eyes of the beloved." I talked about how the Dances of Universal Peace moved me, looking into each other's eyes and seeing the light and love shining through. When I started talking about how I wanted a soul mate, a partner that I can share this with, Neelam stopped me and said "Let's not go there." Everyone laughed, including me. "Just when it starts to get juicy," she smiled.

Neelam clarified that the initial impulse of wanting to connect with the beloved is real. Then it goes into a story when I begin to project it onto a human being. So she asked me to just stay with the longing, and I did. I sat there feeling it fully, this intense pain in my chest. I closed my eyes and let the tears flow. In a few minutes the intensity subsided.

Neelam asked what was arising now. Looking into her eyes, I felt this impersonal love flowing between us, and I said, "I see the beloved in you and in all these eyes." I looked around the room. She asked, "Is that enough?" It was so obvious that what I was longing for was not outside of me. "Yes, of course," I smiled. This love is who I am, is who and what we all are. The longing for that kind of love reminds me to turn within. As Chameli said, "Trust your own original longing."

Still, it was no wonder that Ulli wanted what Annette "has." Annette is radiant. Her deep brown eyes twinkle when she laughs which she does often. There's an intensity about her, but it is not the kind of intensity that pushes you away. Instead it draws you near like a warm fire. We sat in big soft chairs next to each other, where we did the interview in my bedroom.

ഏരു

What stands out about your childhood?

My love for classical music and my connection with nature. I spent a lot of time with animals and in the forest behind my house, and I was talking to God continuously. My mother was Protestant; my father a devout Catholic. My father and I had a strong bond because of our faith while the rest of our family didn't display or show that much of an interest in spiritual matters.

When you were a little girl, how would you describe your relationship with God?

I would have these internal dialogues and, of course, being a child and being brought up in that way, I believed that God was something separate from me, an authority outside myself. Yet it was so intimate. Sometimes there was such an immense feeling of love and devotion, I would enclose myself in my father's office at home, I would light a candle, kneel in front of it, and put my hands together as if praying. It wasn't even a prayer, but I needed to bring a form somehow for this burning in my heart. I was around seven years old.

I remember one day my teacher asked everyone in the class if they believed in God, and one of my best friends said, "God doesn't exist." I came home and asked my mother, "Can you believe that?" To me, it was like saying that I didn't exist. I couldn't put it together how it was possible not to believe.

I remember another interesting event. Somewhere between the age of five and eight, I couldn't sleep. It was summer, it was hot in my room, and I tossed and turned around. I decided to lie completely still to trick myself into sleeping. Suddenly I became aware of "all the words around." I meant the endless stream of thoughts, but I didn't have that word in my vocabulary yet. I wondered, "Where do all these words come from?" Then that stream just stopped, and there was an empty spot, without borders, that expanded. It had a funny feeling to it, like it was sucking me in, dissolving me. Terror rose up, and I shook myself out of it. I quickly folded my hands and prayed, "Please, please God. Never ever stop the words again!"

It had a lasting effect on me because one day much later, my father showed me a picture of the Milky Way and wanted to explain to me about the different galaxies. I was very resistant because the image reminded me of that scary limitless emptiness I had experienced. I told him, "I don't want to know about that."

Fast forward for us to what you would consider a crossroads.

When I was about 21, I felt disconnected from my environment in Germany and the way the people around me seemed to view life and the world. I felt more connected to the southern way—more warmth, heart and a sense of daily celebration. I left my studies at the Conservatory of Music and moved to Spain. Then the depression set in when I was about 24 or 25.

Can you talk about the depression?

I didn't know then what it was about. Obviously, that was part of the depression. I was living and studying in Madrid at the time. The depression was sometimes so strong that for weeks my first thought upon waking up in the morning was, "Oh my God, please, not another day!" What made it worse was that I had a lovely partner, I had friends, and I lived in a place I wanted to live. The outside was apparently perfect, but it was unbearable.

How did it change?

I started therapy, yoga, and t'ai chi intensely three times a week. I experimented with meditation. I went to astrologers and tarot readings. There was a lot of trying to make sense of it, but it was still overwhelming.

As you look back on that now, what's your sense of what was going on?

One aspect might have been that there was a lot of emotional upheaval. There had been sexual molesting in my childhood and an attempted rape from the father of a friend—from persons who were no strangers to me. Also my father was a substance abuser and was sometimes rather severe in his punishments. So, who knows if that was the cause, but there were a few things that confused me a lot, and I didn't know how to deal with it. It's not so much what happens to us, but it's that we don't know how to be with or integrate our experiences.

The other aspect was spiritual. I came to a dead end in a certain way. You see that everything can be perfect circumstances, but inside there is something missing or just not "right." It was funny. I didn't miss God. God for me existed, and yet there was something that didn't make sense.

So, you're saying you felt the presence of God.

Well, yeah, what I labeled as God. There was a strong faith and devotion, but what I didn't understand is that I thought I was this separate someone. "I am separate from this world. I am separate from you. I am separate from God." Now I can formulate it this way. If you would have asked me then, I couldn't have known because no one at that time or in my environment was speaking in such terms or clarifying the misconception.

After some years, the depression got a little bit better, but there was still this sense that there was something I had to find. So I left my life behind when I was 29—my partner, my dog, my friends. I had a good career, I was self-employed, and I lived at the ocean. These were privileged circumstances, and I felt guilty about it. I was supposed to be happy. Yet, all these worldly things didn't have much meaning anymore.

I had this urge to throw myself completely into the world, to travel widely and intensely so I would finally understand what is the essence of life. I had this sense that if I would stretch myself enough, know all the extremes within and without, I would find the common denominator, the answer to the riddle of life.

My partner didn't want me to leave. Some friends said I was nuts, others thought I was ungrateful, but a yoga teacher supported and encouraged me to follow that calling. I was very scared when I left, but I didn't have a choice. I met a few people in India, they were speaking about enlightenment, but I wasn't interested in that concept. I didn't even ask what it meant. I was just interested in following this inner fragrance that was saying, "You follow me, and I will lead you." I stayed almost a year in India, traveling, studying, meeting different people. I also lived and traveled in Nepal, Thailand, Japan, New Zealand, and Australia. I traveled for three years. It was quite an adventure.

So what happened after three years?

It reached a crucial point in Japan in 1997 in the winter. Suddenly, I realized that I had gone through all these different life experiences. I had done all these different things in the world, chasing continuously around to find some answer or a lasting sense of rest. I had had experiences of the fullness of life, the bliss, deep connection, and meeting like-minded people. I had also endured loneliness, fear, and doubt about my journey. I had had different meditative experiences, what people call "openings" like being flooded by lights. But it was never anything that felt like the "real thing," so I didn't give it much attention.

I came to this certain point where a natural inquiry took place. I said to myself, "Hold on a minute. I've done this and that, and it seems to be like dresses I wear and then leave behind. This is Annette scene one, Annette scene two, and all this is changing. If all this is changing, who am I?" I was shocked and thought, "I have lost my mind. I've lost the plot completely!" I couldn't find the "I" that was me! I was extremely upset about it. I didn't have the knowledge that would say, "This is a very good discovery, go on."

Instead it was this feeling, "You are in really big trouble. You left a good life just to go on this crazy journey, believing in God and that everything would be fine, and look where you are now." It was devastating. It came together with states of paranoia where in the morning I didn't want to look in the mirror because I was afraid I wouldn't see my reflection anymore. Upon looking, I was relieved, but then immediately the panic set in again because this body, this face didn't seem to *really* be me.

It felt like my adventurous endeavor was a failure. I looked back and asked, "Where did I make the mistake?" I felt I had done my very best so I decided, "Just call it life and say goodbye." I was ready to finish, commit suicide. It wasn't out of a feeling that my life was all terrible, but I was really tired. There were moments of being concerned about my family. I didn't want to cause them suffering nor have my neighbors find me with blood on the tatami. But my sense of complete alienation from life and the world was stronger.

So, I went through the snow at 2 a.m. to a 24-hour shop to buy some razors. I knew I wouldn't find sleeping pills. I still had a cell phone in my coat pocket from when I had come home before. I touched the cell phone, and there was this thought, "I could call one of my friends and say, 'I need help. I don't know what's going on.'" But it was clear that they wouldn't have the answer. If there's anything that could help me, it must be *That* I had always trusted. So if *That* wouldn't want me to die, it would stop me.

As soon as I arrived at the front of the shop, my phone rang. It was a man's voice. He said, "It's Brett." I didn't remember anyone with that name. He reminded me that we had had coffee together six weeks ago and exchanged phone numbers. He apologized saying this was a terrible time to call anyone, but he had woken up in the middle of the night with an intense feeling he had to call me right now. He was a sensitive and bright person. He said, "I don't know what is happening with you, but I feel you must be in a very difficult space. I want you to come over to my house so you have someone to talk to."

I resisted at first, but then something broke down in me and was relieved. I went into the shop and handed the cell phone over the counter, and Brett gave the man his address and the directions to call a taxi. Half an hour later, I was at his house.

I broke down completely, and I was crying, "I don't know who I am!" Brett looked at me quite puzzled and said, "Well, you're Annette. You were born in Germany. You're studying in the morning, and in the afternoon you work. I think you're a competent person, and you're a beautiful woman." I kept crying, "No, this is not who I am." We didn't get to an understanding, but it was OK. He was very kind and comforting, and something in me gave up. I felt, "OK, *That* made this happen. *That* shall take care of me now." I didn't do anything anymore. It was a hanging out, not even a waiting.

Are you talking about a surrender?

I am not very fond of that word. It can convey a sense of someone "doing" it, and it is not like that. To me, it was an organic development, a choiceless understanding, a simple falling away of trying to control life, reaching for something.

The idea that I'm the one doing life or creating my reality.

Yes, there was not knowing what would happen. A week or two later, a friend from San Francisco called to see if she could visit me in Japan. I told her I didn't know if I would still be here when she came. She suggested we could meet in Australia. "I've done that. I've been there." She wondered if I had been to Byron Bay. After I hung up, it was so strong. I knew I had to go to Byron Bay, and I didn't want to. I was tired of traveling and ending up in new places, but a day later a friend in Australia called. She offered to take me to Byron Bay, so I ended up in Australia a month later.

The very first day on the street in Byron Bay, I met a man who was doing Tibetan eye readings. He looked familiar to me. I asked him if I had met him in India, and he said, "Yeah, yeah, you look familiar," and we chatted. "Come on, I will give you a little eye reading." He looked into my eye and said, "Oh my God, you are so ripe. Look, you have to see a man who's here in town who is doing *satsang*." "*Satsang*, what's that?" He told me it was a spiritual gathering. I said, "No thank you. I'm not interested," but he explained they were meeting in a wooden building, the surf club on the beach.

Somewhere in my head I remembered the conversation because after a few days something got unruly in me and said, "You need to go there." I didn't want to, but I found myself walking towards it like in a daze. There was a gathering of maybe 80 people or so, and someone was playing guitar. After awhile, a man came in. He sat silently for a few minutes, and then he said, "Welcome everyone to *satsang*. Please feel free to speak. We have a microphone that goes around."

People would get the microphone and speak, but the teacher suddenly said, "Excuse me. Give the microphone to this young lady there," and he pointed to me. The microphone came to me, and I felt embarrassed. I didn't have any questions, but something came out of my mouth. "I have this very simple and yet it seems complex question, 'What is all this pain about?'"

He said, "Well, if you have a lot of pain and you have a nightmare, then you want to wake up. If you're dreaming very pleasantly, it's just fine to be asleep. Are you willing to explore something? My experience is that when people come and they have pain or suffering, it all has to do with who they think they are. So I want you to just be open and forget everything you have ever read or heard or perhaps studied that you're a soul, that you're this body or anything. Just for a moment, allow yourself to directly experience who are you?"

When he said these last words, the whole world stopped. It was just complete stillness. Then suddenly the first sound I heard was the ocean crashing against the beach, and I knew immediately, "I am this ocean out there! I am the ocean." I looked at the room which was me as well. "I am the people. I am the chairs. I am the microphone. I am this body." I wanted to say, "I'm everything." As soon as I wanted to utter this, it sort of popped and gave way to limitless transparency, a transparent nothingness that could not be located specifically. Yet everything was made out of that. I couldn't speak anymore.

He asked again, "Hello, who are you? What did you find?" The answer came, "I am everything and nothing." He started to laugh and said, "Yes! That's it. That's it. Wow. That didn't take very long." The next step was, "OK, let's look again. This everything and nothing, do you have to do anything to be that?" "No," I said. It was obvious. It seemed a very silly question.

"OK, let's go back a bit more into the story. You spoke of some pain. Was it emotional pain or physical pain? What was it?" I wanted to tell him about this red thread in my life that felt like a hole in my heart. I looked, and I tried to find some pain, but I couldn't find anything anymore. It was like nothing ever really happened. It was like a dream.

What had happened in that moment was the knowing I am outside of manifestation, prior to the universe and galaxies, never born. Yet I was at the center of everything in creation. This is what I had always been looking for. I was at home. I had never left. It was like a thirty thousand pound backpack dropped. And this laughter deep from my belly swelled up. I laughed and laughed, and the teacher laughed with me.

This teacher was Isaac Shapiro, right? [Annette nods.] Last night you talked about people coming through the back door and others having a big bang kind of awakening. That sounds like a big bang.

I know. This is why I usually don't tell the story because it seems a big bang, a dramatic story. Also, it doesn't end here. It is a beginning.

And are you afraid people will think it has to look like that?

This is always the tricky thing because when people hear certain stories, there is the fascination with the different experiences of someone else, a belief that it should look this or that way. The person, then, is made special. But it is not about the person or one particular way. The most important thing is to ask, "Where do these experiences arise from? What is present already prior to all experiences and is unchanging?" This is what we have to recognize.

So this so-called awakening experience is the beginning. How did it get more refined?

There's an integration or a refinement on many levels. Again, this might be different for someone else. On one hand, there was a shift of perspective, living and operating from a deeper understanding, sometimes being completely awake while the body is deeply asleep, knowing myself as causeless happiness, as the infinite, then sometimes being completely wrapped up in the limits of the personal identity.

Also with time, there was an intense and sometimes truly agonizing emotional clearing. There was no way to hide from my experiences anymore. It felt that things from the past would arise again, be relived, but now there was the opportunity to really be with it and not turn away.

Of course, the world goes on with its demands and needs. We all need to make money, go to the dentist, and so on. I was getting used to undisturbed spaciousness, and at the same time was really opening to the human experience with all its splendor and pain. This opening uncovers the inherent softness of the heart. It is not anything intellectual but a "slipping into place" with all of life which is ordinary and humbling but also exquisite and deeply rewarding.

I remember one day seeing a rotting bird on the beach and being completely overwhelmed by the beauty of it; images of starvation and dying passing through—all that we see as horrible. In that moment, I saw it as the unfathomable beauty that is me. At the same time, I am increasingly sensitive to all the suffering that exists.

Can you give us an example of something painful that you could be with?

After that shift of perspective, I had a boyfriend who left me. I was in pain about it because I didn't wish the relationship to end, but I could see that my pain was actually made out of many components like, "What will other people think? What does this mean about me?" It was seeing that all those thoughts were imposters in a certain way, movements away from what *is*. Then pain was simply flushing through my chest, clean pain or sadness without stickiness. Beautiful.

It seems like a good time to talk about relationships.

Before, my relationships were all about "me." How do I get love. How do I get what I need? It was a sort of bargaining or trading. Now, love is something very different. It stands on its own—without cause. It is not about trying to change someone so he fits my perspective. Sharing my life with others and my partner is a gift. It enriches my life. It's "how God loves God" in daily experience. Usually when something comes up that doesn't seem to be in alignment in our relationship, we can look at it without blaming or making each other wrong. We hold the space for it, and let it be. Usually there is a gift in it. It is an invitation to an endless deepening, a returning to real innocence and humanness.

Is he on some kind of a path?

He has been in a Sufi community for many years, but he also has a background in Vipassana and Zen.

Does he participate in satsang?

He's been to a few other teachers. We don't speak much about it. We don't theorize much. It's simply the living of it.

Has he had what you would call this shift?

I don't know. I don't classify people as awake or not awake. My essence and his essence are the same. It's simple: "You are *This*. This cup of tea is *This*." I find it misleading to speak of awakening. It sounds like a happening.

Last night you said the feminine leans towards fullness. What is it about the feminine, not women, that's different?

To me, it's a distinctive aspect of reality. The feminine is the aspect of energy, the pulse of life, I experience as creation in its fullness. It is also the aspect of interconnectedness that is intrinsic in empathy and openness towards life's experiences. In India they call it Shakti. Shiva represents more the aspect of unmoving emptiness of space. "Shiva is nothing without Shakti," says the *Bhagavad Gita*. We all, men and women, are made out of both and are invited to recognize ourselves as those sacred principles. They are different aspects of reality, but not separate.

The feminine principle is also about the evoking of beauty. "She" is always present when someone decorates a house, creates harmony or art. Women generally like to adorn themselves. It doesn't come necessarily from egoic vanity or to attract a partner. It is an overflow of the radiance of our hearts and the need to bring that out. The world needs that, especially in difficult times. It is the reflection that says "everything is sacred."

What do you share in your satsang *that brings forth more of the feminine than a masculine embodiment would?*

When I do meetings for men and women, I now call them "Circles of Presence." I prefer a more interactive participation, a more lateral sharing. I see myself rather as a facilitator, not a teacher.

We can easily fall into the trap of using concepts of spirituality to escape or be dishonest with ourselves about what is going on in our lives. We can even use silence and emptiness to try and compensate for our difficulty to connect with other people or engage in life. We might be trying to integrate silent presence in daily life, but the experiential aftermath of some past events make it difficult. I find it important to attend to that. Otherwise, it keeps creating a painful split and intellectual pretentiousness rather than a real and heart-felt integration.

I observe in some Advaita circles a tilt towards the Absolute, like a clinging to emptiness which results in an unwillingness to attend to the personal and human aspects. It reminds me of the old stories of religion in which the body and the worldly existence were considered a nuisance to be left behind. Women tend to be more grounded in that aspect and more connected to life. As Papaji, the Indian sage and teacher, once said,

"Realized men set up a religion. Realized women return home to the hearth and the family."

Can you talk more about the women's circles?

I have felt for many years the strong pull to bring women together. Central to the gathering is to recognize and give space to what is already whole and precious in us. Otherwise we keep repeating the old stories, trying to fill the holes in our hearts through endless shopping, hiding behind immaculate make-up, or imitating men to feel powerful.

The women's circle is a lot about coming back to the body, to its intrinsic wisdom and uncontrived aliveness. Part of it is through dancing, the invitation to dance how we rarely dance—from the present moment, from "within"—to let move what wants to move. We all think too much in our culture. Through movement, stuck energy can flow freely and re-organize itself in the organism. In dance, you can experience this very cellular knowing, opening up to the reality that it's all energy. It's all a dance.

Another part of the gathering might be sharing of the challenges of daily life. Women can support each other by simply listening. To be received without analysis or without someone trying to fix you is a gift in itself.

Your teacher said that you're not going to wake up from a good dream, so do you have to have a bad dream? Do you have to have a dark night of the soul?

No. That's a concept that can foster ideas of postponement and misunder-standing. A dark night of the soul might have been the case for some of us, but non-dual awareness, the silent Self, is already present. Always.

Is there anything else important to share?

I want to end with a dedication: "May we all breathe, walk and talk from preciousness and infinity."

₧₨

Annette had a private session scheduled after the interview, so she and Francie left for town. The sun was shining when they drove off the mesa but before long, a spring snowstorm moved in, and it began to really dump. I sat at my desk looking outside at the big fat flakes, and started to write in my journal:

> *Annette's story of how she "woke up" really is seductive, I have to confess. My mind locks onto the story and thinks that's the way it's supposed to look. It can't help itself. The mind wants to figure this out. And it thinks that if it just does it a certain way, follows a particular formula, then I will "get" it. But there is no "I" to get it. And there's no formula. Like Anandimaya Ma said, "There are six billion ways."*
>
> *It was in the kitchen during a break when Annette looked at me and said, "There is no way the mind can do this because the mind wants to have it, to own it. And there is no such thing to have." Tears came to my eyes when she said that. I knew it was true.*
>
> *It's like using my hands to grasp some air to breathe. The air is right here, it's available. If I try too hard to breathe, it's like a panic attack. But if I just relax, breathing happens without effort. Our true nature will naturally arise because it is right here. Always.*

The phone rang, and it was Annette and Francie on their cell phone. It was dark by then. They were lost and stuck in their two-wheel drive rental car somewhere on the mesa. Chris and I bundled up and headed out in the storm with a tow rope and chains, items we always keep in the truck in the winter. After a quick search nearby, there was no sign of them, no tracks in the snow, no headlights. The wind was blowing, and it was still snowing making visibility near zero. We called on our cell phone to try and determine their location. "We can see someone's car lights behind us. Is that you?" Since we couldn't see them we knew it must be someone else. "Maybe you can stop them and ask where you are."

It was a neighbor who got on the phone and told us their exact location. We drove for a few more minutes and found the little car in the middle of the road on a slight hill, unable to go forward. With my winter driving experience and Chris's pushing power, we managed to get the car turned around and back down the hill to a safe location for the night. We all piled into the cab of the truck and drove home, the snow still coming down hard. Once inside, we gathered around the woodstove and laughed about what could now be called "a mesa adventure."

As they warmed up around the fire, I told Francie and Annette about my women's group that has been meeting for almost ten years, how we celebrate the seasons and cycles of the year, creating our own earth-based ceremonies. There's a sense of shared responsibility because we take turns leading the group. Movement, deep listening, silence, and creativity are all components of our regular gatherings.

When they left the following day, Francie and Annette expressed a genuine desire to return sometime as guests of our women's group. It was obvious they believed we had something to offer to them, another reminder that there is no hierarchy except for what we create in our heads. It occurred to me that not only are love and peace available right here, right now; wisdom is also available. All aspects of our true nature.

Francie Halderman

Francie was born in California in 1963, the youngest of five kids. She grew up in Kentucky in what she describes as a blue-collar family. Trained as a nurse, she now works in a pain management practice in Philadelphia. She was asked by Pamela Wilson to give *satsang* in 2003.

CHAPTER 9

FRANCIE HALDERMAN

I really wanted to know how this is lived,
how in the nitty-gritty, the business world,
parenting, relationships, in all aspects,
how is this lived?

I first met Francie at Pamela's spring retreat in northern New Mexico. I remember saying I wanted to be just like her when I grew up. I wasn't kidding. She was soft, sweet, and awake.

Francie and Annette had separate bedrooms when they stayed at my house, but the first morning I could hear the two of them in the upstairs room giggling like teenagers at a slumber party. I tentatively knocked on the door and found them still in their pajamas working on a laptop computer, creating their next workshop. I joined them for a while, sitting on the bed chatting for a few minutes before we fixed breakfast and prepared for the gathering at the house that day.

During the meditation time at the beginning of *satsang*, there it was again; that familiar resistance to give up the little me. "I like my life. I'm having fun. Why should I let this go?" The answer came from within, "You don't have to. The mountain doesn't care if you walk on top of it. This vastness doesn't care if you are attached to a separate self." There's no agenda in consciousness, so there's really nothing to resist.

The opposite of resistance is acceptance. Once I welcomed the desire to have a separate little self, there was this big sigh of relief. It makes no difference whether I resist or not anyway. It is inevitable that we will return, and we will awaken to our true nature. There's no choice about that. It's like a child who refuses to come home when Mom calls. She knows that the kid has to come home. There's really no place else to go. The kid knows it but is just playing a little game. No need to get upset or take it all too seriously.

I shared some of these insights with the circle gathered in my living room for the day. The weather was perfect for the event—not too snowy and not too sunny, so people weren't tempted to go skiing instead. I put a lot of energy into getting folks to attend these events. I knew that I shouldn't care who was there or who wasn't there, but it was hard not to take it personally when some of my good friends didn't show up.

The next morning, I read in one of my Advaita books that it is not only inevitable we return, but the timing of the return or Self-realization is predestined. If that is true, then it is easy to let go of all expectation around what others are doing—or not. What a relief, not only for me but for them, too. Instantly, I was able to accept the fact that one of my best friends chose not to participate. It was none of my business. I never said anything about it to her. Later I noticed there was no more tension in the air between us when I shared with her about *satsang*. She was politely interested, and that was fine. I thought, "If only I can be this accepting about Chris and his participation!"

೫೦೫೮

Can you reflect on what was unique about your childhood?

There was immense pain in my family. My Mom was severely depressed, which later turned into an anxiety disorder. My oldest brother had a drug problem, and he eventually committed suicide. There was a lot of yelling in the family, a lot of frustration. My father was very temperamental and would hit my oldest brother, so there was a fair amount of verbal and some physical violence that happened. We lived between two farms. I was able to go out in the woods, sometimes for a day at a time and just be in nature which was really a saving grace.

I remember around the age of 12, I woke up in the middle of the night, and there was this not knowing who I was, the boundaries had slipped away. It resulted in a panic in the body. That was the concrete start of a lot of anxiety episodes, a sort of flooding sensation. I was functional. Most people from the outside wouldn't even know it. This occurred throughout high school and into adulthood a little bit.

When I was around age 14, I was sitting in 9th grade chemistry class and we were reviewing one of the laws of physics which stated "neither matter nor energy can be created nor destroyed; *it can only change form.*" I remember being totally stunned and recognizing, "Oh my God, there is some aspect of me, everyone, and everything that *always is,* and wasn't born, and can't die!" Instead of having a concept of what is eternal, there was an *experience* of knowing that everything is connected, and the body started to relax around issues of anxiety and death.

What else about those early years contributed to how you got "here"?

There weren't a lot of expectations in the family. Education wasn't really on the radar screen. I had always loved education and felt very different from the rest of my family, like I didn't belong. I didn't have enough confidence or money to go to college, so I went to a vocational school at age 17, an LPN program which was actually very thorough. When I started my nursing career in Cincinnati, I saw people from all walks of life, all different social classes. Illness is the great leveler. In those years of bedside nursing, my patients were my teachers.

Shortly after I graduated from LPN school, I became pregnant with the child of the man I was dating for several years. This was completely unplanned but a joyous and beautiful pregnancy. My first experience with what I would now call "this great emptiness" was in labor. I really felt a sense that "life is moving through me." When your body is doing this contraction, there's clearly nothing *you* are doing. In between the contractions, I noticed I would drop down into this emptiness. It was empty, yet there was an immense presence.

Four months after the birth of my daughter, I thought I was pregnant again. The doctor's office didn't think I needed to come in for a visit, but there was something in me that insisted, so I came in for an exam. They said I wasn't pregnant but a small cervical erosion which was present after delivery had grown incredibly, and the doctor wanted to do a biopsy.

I found out the results by reading them in the car because the doctor didn't have the guts to tell me. It was invasive cancer. Initially the doctor told me on the phone the cancer was pre-invasive, but when I read it was a different stage than the doctor told me, I knew immediately it meant the loss of my fertility, no more children and radical surgery. Survival at that time was about 60 per cent meaning 40 percent of the people with this stage die.

One gift of this reproductive cancer was the chance at a young age to deeply explore what it means to be female. Becoming a young mother, assuming all the associated responsibilities, and loving all of it—only to permanently lose my child-bearing abilities so soon at age 20—was very hard. It allowed me to really sit and ask, "What is the essence of being a woman?"

Another gift was really living every moment. Here I had this new life, this daughter, Andrea, who was beautiful and incredible. While she wasn't planned, I saw the wisdom of it. If I hadn't had her then, I possibly never would have had a child. There was an immense gratitude for almost every moment, whether it was stressful or incredibly beautiful. Knowing she would be the only one, I really savored it and attended to it. You know, like the dishes can stay in the sink for now.

In a curious way, the loss of my fertility was almost harder to deal with than the possibility of dying. I would have loved to have had two or three more children, perhaps not with my husband at the time. He couldn't deal with the cancer. He was limited in his capacity to participate in the marriage in general.

In what other ways did the experience of having cancer affect you?

There was the burning question, "Why?" My oncologist was great. Very succinctly he asked, "Francie, why does a two-year-old get a brain tumor?" That was such a gift because the "why" instantly dropped.

Also, there was more compassion in my nursing. You just become very aware of the subtleties, like if you're in a hospital bed and a door slams. I feel like I was sensitive and caring before my own diagnosis, but afterwards there was an extra availability I had in being with people.

You haven't talked about any kind of a more structured spiritual path.

After my divorce, I met a male nurse who worked on the adolescent psyche unit. That was my first exposure to someone who was a seeker. He showed me Joseph Campbell tapes. I was watching them when I was alone, and the message that was on these tapes, I remember my jaw dropping. I had been raised Catholic. My father was very strict. To hear that God is already within me and in everything was blasphemy. Even then, there was this experience, "God is everywhere and is everything."

A couple of years later, I started going to my friend's teacher in Colorado who taught consciousness studies from a bio-psychological perspective. We intensively studied evolutionary psychology, formation of character, and sensory awareness. It was my first exposure to not trusting the "story" that goes on in the mind so much because we looked at the relationship of what forms character and affects perception. There are so many components.

After a few years, I learned what I needed to learn, and I felt I had "worked on myself" enough. I could see the shunning of students who did not see things exactly as this teacher did, and I decided to trust my inner voice that was arising opposed to his. I started dating a man I later married who was also a student in that group. When I quit the group, he continued studying for a while, and I saw him get tangled in the "group think" dynamics of it all and suffer. I was pretty "anti-teacher" because of this.

Another event that happened around that time in my life was a major car accident and head injury. I was knocked unconscious in a head-on collision which resulted in an open skull fracture, concussion, and cervical disc herniations. I was off work for four months recuperating, struggling with short term memory loss and slight speech issues. This really helped me sit with the question, "OK, *now* who am I?" as someone temporarily without normal physical capabilities and, in some ways, without my normal intellect. What is left here?

Back to the time you met your future husband—it sounds like he was more into the spiritual path than you were at the time.

In 1994, I moved to Philadelphia, and we got married in '98. He still very much felt the seeking, and I was skeptical to say the least. I didn't want him to get hurt anymore. I didn't want him getting involved in groups where he would end up feeling worse about himself, but he continued to go to teachers and different kinds of groups. I gave him a hard time about it partly because he was gone a lot, and there was that whole relationship dynamic, "Don't you just want to be with me?" When he came back, and I think I was seeing it pretty objectively, he would have a sense of relief, but it seemed to feed into the idea that more work needed to be done.

And how did that affect you?

I guess it sort of inoculated me against more teachers.

But then along comes Pamela Wilson.

My husband would have phone sessions with Pamela. It was easier for him to tell me that they were career counseling sessions. That seemed OK somehow. [She laughs.] He said, "France, you should meet her. She's really different. I think you would like her." So I sat with that for about a year maybe.

Meanwhile, when I moved to Philadelphia, I was hired by a national health care company in administration and started getting a string of promotions. Before I knew it, I was a national director of nursing in a company with forty-four thousand employees. I hadn't been seeking any of this. I had no formal executive skills to draw upon, but I strangely knew what to do and how to maneuver. I really felt the sense of something *moving through* me. There could be no claim that "I" achieved this position.

It was my job to create a nationwide program for quality management for all our sites and lines of service. A large component of this was to reduce medical errors and mistakes. I created a non-punitive error reporting program which was a huge leap to propose at that time. And it worked.

I was asked to write articles in peer review journals and received awards. I got on the lecture circuit illustrating how we did this in our company and changed the culture. The whole time I felt that this really was not my path. I was grateful, but I didn't want to put my ladder up on the wrong wall so to speak.

Then I started having a health condition. My intestines started to twist. I couldn't be too far from medical care because if my intestines twisted again and didn't untwist, obviously I would need surgery. I tried a lot of self-care to avoid the surgery. It was at that point, I was 39 years old, that I decided to quit my job.

About three months after that my husband said, "You know, Pamela is coming to town. You might really want to meet her." I remembered she had done career counseling sessions, a little trick of omission that my husband didn't clarify. [She laughs.] So I thought, "This is great because I really want to get clear on what I want to do with my life." I had a private session with Pamela, instantly resonated with her, and could see there was no agenda. She was very sweet in how she started the session: "This is just friends sitting with friends. What would you like to talk about?" I said, "Clarity." Pamela replied, "Excellent."

Very soon into the session I felt myself disappear and yet felt that presence of being there. I asked Pamela, "What was this! What happened? I have a feeling when I walk out the door; it will all be back to the same."

She said, "You don't know that." And I listened.

I went to one *satsang* after that and profoundly saw the essence of who we are beyond our roles of individual persona. I could see the personal identity was on the surface "trying to be somebody," how sweet and innocent that was and how completely unnecessary. Soon after, Pamela was having a week-long retreat in New Mexico, and I went to that. Then things started to fall away that weren't needed. Again, I felt this "emptiness with presence" and this well-being, nothing fancy, certainly no extreme bliss that a lot of people felt.

With Pamela, there was this beautiful invitation to welcome everything. It was at her retreat in the middle of the night that I woke up, and this old panic, this old anxiety from childhood started to arise. Immediately there was this sense of welcoming it, really inviting it in. As soon as I did, I felt myself shrink, even smaller than a dot. There was this sensation of opening up. A lot of what wasn't necessary just fell away. That's all I can say to describe it. Again, you have to understand that just a month before, I was a complete skeptic. I couldn't believe it.

The second night my husband had come to join me, and he was fast asleep from jet lag. I experienced this beautiful spirit washing through me over and over. I kept trying to wake my husband up, but he was not to be awakened. The question arose, "Is this one spirit or more than one [multiple spirits]?" Immediately in asking the question, there was a knowing that this was beyond any notion of one or more than one, beyond is or isn't. All those things in Eastern philosophy that sound cryptic or don't make sense— I suddenly *knew* them. Form is emptiness, and emptiness is form. I understood it without thought and without words. It was beyond all categories of thought.

Duality dropped away with that. It was so natural. I rarely tell people about what happened at the retreat because the mind innocently tries to compare. I tell it now with the caveat of the six billion ways. No one should look to anyone else's experience and think, "I haven't felt that. What's wrong with me because I haven't had this big bang?" I know others where it's just been a really subtle contentment without anything apparent, or exploding. It's the same. I really invite people not to get distracted with the story.

There were six months of nirvana, which would be my word. When you read the definition of it, that's pretty much how I would describe that period.

But you say it wasn't blissful?

For me, I would describe it as very ordinary, simple well-being. That's probably a blessing because I am quite sure I would have confused the bliss with the *It*. The *It* that can't be named. I probably would have continued to seek and cling to that bliss state again. Instead, this was seeing *It* in every-thing that arose—bliss, angst, the whole spectrum was included.

Absolutely everything is part of the Divine and underneath everything is love. I could see behavior in another person and immediately I would see the pain or ignorance behind and even underneath that, a desire to love.

Maybe it was a function of not having been involved in spiritual circles before, but it was so funny to me when I would hear some people talk about being awake or not awake. I could see how that concept itself created more seeking, more struggle, more suffering. It's so innocent because the mind is only trying to be the "freedom coach," yet it's the wrong instrument. The mind is a reducing valve as Joe Campbell said. While all the wisdom and love in the universe is already inside us all, only the heart can know this. It's just too big for the rational mind to grasp. It's really getting comfortable with "knowing I don't know" and resting in this simple mystery which is to be lived, not a problem to be solved. The heart knows the way and can be trusted.

After the six months of nirvana, what happened?

I went back into helping the family business, a pain management practice, which had a lot of financial problems. Some of the employees had stolen money so the practice was in jeopardy. When I realized someone was stealing money from us, the initial thing that welled up was laughter because I could see that he was playing a role, and the theft required a response. My husband and I were playing a role in getting an attorney, but it is not *who we are*.

Then I was back in the hospital with an intestine episode which would not untwist on its own and was becoming gangrenous. Despite really trying to avoid surgery, it was necessary. My husband was out of town and the doctor was waiting for him to come back to do the surgery. I was going on my third day of no sleep, having been in pain, and I was in a holding area on a stretcher awaiting surgery. There was some confusion between the hospital floor and the ER suite, and I was left alone in a hallway for four hours unmedicated.

It was pure bliss. I had always had a very high pain tolerance, but in this situation, I could not have been conscious and had more pain. There was this emptiness, yet there was also a presence there. That's the best way I can describe it. The pain was present, but what was so strongly arising was gratitude for this part of my intestine that had served me for 40 years. It wasn't like an exercise; it was just spontaneous gratitude, thanking it for all of its service, loving it, loving my body.

There was a moment when the mind started to think of all the possibilities of what could happen in the operation because there had been some concern that this was a reoccurrence of the cancer. Then I saw how beautiful the mind was. It knew that I was about ready to be cut open, and it had the wisdom to know this was necessary, to know this was going to happen, and to not freak out, jump off the table and run away. I had this awe for my mind, how noble it was.

It was a revelation because I really got it that if I had moved to freak out, it would have been love, too. That would have been just as amazing as these four hours where I was in bliss awaiting surgery. Again, how innocently all of us seek certain experiences when *either way*, it's the same.

It's the same Source which is love. So right here and now, right where you are, this is the holy land, and this is the holy moment.

Two weeks after my surgery, I went to work. The body hadn't even recovered, and I was working 10 to 12 hour days, Saturdays included, to help the family business keep from going under. I really wanted to know how *This* is lived, how in the nitty-gritty-shitty, the business world, relationship, in all aspects, how *This* is lived.

How is "This" lived in relationships? Has your relationship with your husband changed as a result of your own experience?

Well, my current relationship with my husband is in transition. Back when all of this was occurring, when I would see a sort of reaction arise in him or anyone, there was instant compassion. It wasn't a practice or a sense that I need to find this compassion, it was there because I saw where his reaction came from. In my not reacting back, grace dissolves her own creation. Truly, that's with everything.

Here's your husband who has done all this seeking and you who weren't even seeking but have apparently found it. What a paradox.

This may sound totally unrelated, but I think it is relevant. I saw a documentary made in the 1950s called *Her Eyes Were Blue*. It was about a teacher in a small rural town who did an experiment about racism. It speaks to the innocence of what we tell ourselves and what we expect. It also relates to the idea of awake or not-awake. She said to the students, "We have done research, and we now know that all people with blue eyes are smarter than people with brown eyes, so all the people with blue eyes come over here." Very subtly through language and other ways, this was reinforced for several weeks.

The IQ of the children with brown eyes actually dropped. The children started treating the brown-eyed kids really badly on the playground. Then she reversed the experiment. She told them after a period of a few weeks, "We found out we were wrong. Now we know for sure that people with *brown* eyes are smarter." The IQ started to rise in the brown-eyed children and lowered in the blue-eyed kids. It clearly illustrates the innocence of whatever we're told, we take on.

The way you said it yesterday in our circle was, "There is no such thing as awakening."

When I sit with people, there is a gentle ferociousness not to let anyone think otherwise, that they aren't already what they are seeking. Again, it's friends sitting with friends, no hierarchy. A lot of it is just debunking spiritual myths and inquiring into notions or expectations of how things should look or be.

When I approach people this way, amazing things start to happen. For example, they start to speak to things they were experiencing directly right out of the Upanishads although they had never heard of them before. The same wisdom was already inside them, you see? One after the other, they got the experience of it being here [she points to her heart]. It's not the person in the front of the room, it's everywhere.

The part that seems different in your case is that right before you went to see Pamela, your life was pretty settled. There wasn't anything in particular you were looking for.

Joseph Campbell tells the Grail story of the Knights of the Roundtable who were on a quest to find something in the forest. As they approached the edge of the forest, each knight chose the place to enter that was darkest to them. They considered it a disgrace to enter in *someone else's path*. I so resonate with that. There are six billion plus people, and there is no formula. Just look afresh without "knowing" anything and follow the heart and what you really resonate with.

One last question… can you talk about the uniqueness of the feminine expression in satsang?

My experience is similar to a few other women who give *satsang* or dialogues. One spoke about growing up in the south as a woman with certain expectations of how she should be or act. As an adult she found Tibetan Buddhism only to realize that yet another set of expectations on how to be or act were being imposed. In myself and other women there is now an embracing of the full expression of life in its full range.

As women, we don't have to adopt a notion of emptiness or stillness that diminishes our outward expression of creativity. We can dance, cry with joy or pain, or be drenched in passion. Real freedom allows us to give up even spiritual notions of how we are supposed to "be." We can stay fresh with what is true for us, as women, which is a new offering to the world formerly run by a patriarchal view.

The female aspect is one of inclusion, but it has a sword, too. I recently had an image of myself being able to hold a baby in one arm and simultaneously with the other arm hit an intruding burglar over the head with a two-by-four.

Woman is the knower and giver of forms. Since form equals emptiness, there is no need to push away phenomenon. In many cultures the goddess of sex and creation is also the god of destruction. There is no life without this life/death/life cycle. When you make friends with this you see that death is never the end. It is always followed by new life.

ೞೞ

The interview ended somewhat abruptly when the power in our house went off. We live off-grid which means we produce our own electricity from alternative sources—the sun and wind. Chris was doing some maintenance work and didn't realize he had hit the breaker switch for our room. It was good timing since Annette and Francie had to leave for their next engagement in Aspen.

I took a short cross-country ski across the rolling mesa after they left. It felt good to move, to be outside, to experience the openness of nature. I got into a smooth rhythm of legs and arms, skis and poles, left and right.

When I thought about Francie's story, I had to laugh out loud. She wasn't looking for anything. She thought she was talking to a career counselor when she met with Pamela! How can that be? How can she have this experience of awakening when she wasn't even searching? She didn't *do* anything. What an important lesson—this is so clearly out of our personal control. If we are going to wake up, we are going to wake up. We can't know when. In the meantime, we can only be present with what is. I heard Francie say, "*This* is the holy moment. *This* is the holy land." I stopped skiing and looked around me. Wow, so much beauty. Life as it is. In that moment, it was enough.

ဆဃ

About a month later, I went backpacking with Ulli, a kind of a spring tradition. This year we chose to visit the Grand Canyon—a place of such awe and beauty, no doubt that this is the "holy land"! Each day before dinner, I wrote a little in my journal:

> *Day One. It's so different to be down inside the canyon instead of on top looking at it from above. How else can you know a landscape, know anything if you don't get inside it? And the Grand Canyon is like no other landscape. It's a cliché to say that, but it is a cliché for a reason. I have hiked hundreds of canyons in my life, but no other place carries such a depth of mystery and history (literally!). The creation of the planet comes to life here. It's tangible. Eons of time are visible in the layers the river has carved—is still carving every moment.*
>
> *Day Two. We hiked from our base camp down to the river today. It's hard to believe such a sleepy, insignificant flow of water could create*

such a complex system of canyons. Then I think that the force that carves the canyon is the same force that is shaping my life, the force that is my life. No, not "my" life. It's life. And it's not just the river that created the canyon. All the factors had to be just right—the rate and direction at which the earth was tilting in relation to the rate of the river's flow. All the layers that were laid down before the river was even born. The creation of the planet itself. The creation of the solar system before that. It's too much for the mind to really grasp. Like when I gazed at the starry sky so many years ago.

Day Three. As the days unfold, the magic of the canyon is working on me. It takes time to unwind. My mind is finally at rest. Right now I let myself be absorbed into the awesome vastness. This is no empty void. These are not dead, inanimate rocks. I can really feel the pulsing of life, a kind of warm presence. I melt into the stillness.

Day Four. It is our last evening inside the guts of the earth. I look above me and see the long trail climbing up and out. But that's for tomorrow. Right now, I can just sit here quietly and gaze on the layers upon layers of rocks and remember how Francie described her labor pains. In between contractions, she experienced an emptiness that was filled with an "immense presence." I feel that here.

For the first time, I am making friends with emptiness. In fact, I feel a certain benevolence in all this vastness. It's not like God or some kind of entity. It's bigger than that. Much bigger. It's the Source of all—the opposite of creation. When I think of it that way, it's not so scary anymore. Instead, the void is rich with potential, the promise of life.

Day Five. Not much time to write after an 11-hour day on the trail. The moon is up now, and we can see the glimmer of the Colorado River four thousand feet below us as we prepare a fresh salad in the camper, perched on the edge of the cliff. I am exhausted but in a full, satisfied way.

Back home. I am remembering Adya asking the group at the recent intensive, "What do you notice when you look inside for the 'me'?" I turned within and for a split second I realized that there was nothing there. What a shock. In that very moment, there was a loud crack and thunder shook the building. I literally jumped out of my seat as did everyone else in the room.

It's "all for nothing," Adya laughed. He explained that he uses the word "nothing" to refer to this mystery within because then the mind can't get too grabby about it. If we imagine the mystery is love or peace or bliss, we start looking for it, and we can get stuck in the wanting-something-to-be-different.

In the Grand Canyon, I touched the heart of emptiness and know that it is the essence and the Source of all things, including "me." That's one way to say that I am nothing and everything at the same time. Isn't that what Annette discovered, too? Now it makes more sense.

Neelam

Neelam was born in Poland in 1963. Her passion for t'ai chi took her to Germany and then to America. In 1994, she traveled to India to be with Papaji—and to realize the truth of who she was. In 1996, Papaji gave his blessing to Neelam to offer Satsang. In 2003, she moved to Hotchkiss, Colorado where she is living and starting a community. She travels extensively giving Satsang to small groups throughout Europe, India, and the States. [Neelam has asked that 'Satsang' be used throughout her interview.]

CHAPTER 10

NEELAM

You don't need to wake up,
you don't need to be enlightened,
you don't need to be anything,
because you already are!

It was with Neelam that Pamela had her recognition. I was happily surprised to learn that Neelam had recently moved to western Colorado—right in my backyard. So I have attended several of her Satsang intensives. Neelam's message is simple: to really be here. She often asks, "What is *really* going on? What is it that you are not wanting to be with?" She explains that it's our "story" that keeps us from being here, the way we interpret the circumstances of our life.

At my first Satsang with Neelam, I did an exercise with a partner. Neelam asked us to talk about something that was causing us pain, something that was bothering us. I talked about my frustration with the conditions at the nursing home where I was volunteering. I told my partner how the staff didn't speak much English, so they couldn't communicate clearly with the elderly woman I was taking care of.

The next step was to ask, "What is under the story?" I noticed a tightness in my belly, and I realized it was fear. What kind of fear? Fear of my own ageing process and how I would be treated when I get old. Neelam asked, "Are you willing to sit with that, just make room for it?" I did. The minute I turned towards the real feeling, something softened. There was a sense of relief, a few tears. The fear didn't go away, but it was less intense.

If you wander off track in Satsang, Neelam firmly but gently brings you back: "Let's not go there, sweetheart." This is not an empty term of endearment. She is sincerely inviting you to be tender with yourself, to end the self-criticism. Sometimes she rests her hand on her heart when she speaks. Neelam meets you where you are. If you need emotional support, she goes there. If you need clarification for the mind, she provides that. In her retreats, she includes dancing and movement, too.

There's a way that Neelam is more reserved than some of the other women I interviewed. It helps remind me that it's not about personalities. This awareness-that-we-are comes in all different flavors. We did the interview at a friend's house in Telluride the day after Neelam offered Satsang to our community. Neelam's presence has a kind of calming effect on me, whether in a group or alone. I feel seen, like she can look right into my soul. Presence meeting presence.

ಔಞ

What is it like for you now to talk about your childhood, your "story"?

It is something that I remember, but it's not something that I relate to. I don't have that real sense of engagement with it. When telling the story of the past, some of it is more emotional or alive, but it doesn't have the same hold.

Knowing that, can you think of what stands out that led you to where you are now?

I had a rather normal childhood. There wasn't anything dramatic about it. I do remember experiences of being aware of consciousness. When I was about nine years old, I was away from my parents for the first time on a vacation camp. I got really sick, and I had what I call now an awakening experience where the mind stopped, and there was just a simple connection with what is. That stayed with me for awhile, but it eventually faded. There was no reference point for me to connect it with nor was there anybody I could talk to about it in any way. Yet there was a sense since that things were not the way they seemed. Things were different.

Was there any kind of a turning point when you made a commitment to be on a spiritual search?

As I look back on it, everything was part of that search. There wasn't anything other than that. But there was this time when I moved to Germany, I was studying t'ai chi, and I was reading some of the writings of the old masters that struck a chord of recognition. That's what I really wanted. Still it wasn't really so clear until I came to the States, and I started to study t'ai chi with my Chinese master. While I was doing that, I suddenly went to this place of awakening, and I started to realize what was going on. There was a more conscious search to really undo suffering, to look and say, "There's something going on in me. I don't understand it, but it's very powerful, and I want to find some answers."

It seems like a lot of your motivation was to end suffering.

It was a recognition of how painful it is to be here. It wasn't about anything in particular, but there was a series of awakenings and insights into the nature of reality. Some part of me was really terrified, not knowing what it was. At the same time, I was feeling very acute suffering.

At some point you made a decision to go to India.

I was a devotee of Mother Meera for a couple of years. I read Ramana Maharshi and that really resonated with me, but it seemed like I had to have a teacher in the body. Mother Meera didn't speak, but she was available in that very subtle way providing guidance from inside. I spent this intense time sitting in bliss for hours.

At the same time, the moment I would stop meditating, stop sitting, there was tremendous suffering. So I would go back and forth between this very blissful state and this very painful state of being here. I remember lying down at some point, and a thought arose in me that said, "I want to find someone who can show me out of this because I know there has to be something beyond this."

Soon after that I found myself in Satsang. I didn't know anything about it. Someone brought Gangaji's flyer to our house, and I thought, "That sounds interesting. It's a Western woman. She didn't spend years in a monastery." So I went to Satsang, and that was really powerful and amazing... to drop out of the mind, drop out of the story, and really start to rest. As I was sitting in Satsang with Gangaji, I realized I needed to go see Papaji in India.

At that time, a lot of past desire for things arose, starting a family or maybe doing something else. Then Papaji came to me in a dream, and he gave me a yellow rose and said, "Cut through the dream." So it's hard to say that a decision was made. It was just very, very obvious that I needed to be there.

Tell us about your experience with Papaji.

It's really difficult to describe because the silence is so powerful, to meet someone who actually is that which you are seeking. It's very rare, and the knowing of it is instantaneous. It doesn't happen in the mind. You just know. It was really powerful to sit in his presence. It was amazing to have that grace of Satsang. He was so clear, so direct, and at the same time, so available. There was no doubt in my mind that what he spoke was the truth. Once that happens in consciousness, something changes inside. There's no more of that questioning... is it true or not true. [She is silent.] It's really hard to speak about it.

What do you think is important to share about your experience of so-called awakening?

First of all, there is this level of trust that happens. Over time, you start to trust the teaching as it is. Once that happened for me, then there was this recognition. In one of the Satsang, I asked Papaji if I could come and sit close to him, and when I sat there I realized that everything he was saying was true. In that moment something let go. Something wasn't searching anymore.

I remember going out to dinner that night with my husband at the time and before we left I had this tremendous fear arise, a fear of dying. Nevertheless, we decided to go out and have dinner. As we were walking back to our home, there were these three young Indian girls who came up to me, and they each had a flower. Without saying anything, they each gave me this little flower. That really broke my heart, something opened. I went back home, and I just sat. I decided to allow that fear to be present.

What happened—it was very quick, it took maybe a second, but it takes a long time to describe. There was this fear of dying, and there was this desire to run to Papaji and just sit at his feet. And there was this willingness to surrender. I could feel it just coming over. The room disappeared. Everything I could see with my eyes just disappeared in that moment. And there was this tremendous resting I can't even describe. I can't use words for that.

I don't know how long it lasted. There's no recollection of time. I can only remember the coming back from that experience, the awareness of this body, the awareness of this place where I was sitting. There was tremendous bliss, just incredible bliss and joy, which is only an after-effect; it has nothing to do with true reality, and the deep recognition that every-thing was OK just the way it is. Everything is taken care of. Everything is just perfectly OK the way it is.

That experience changed my life. There's nothing I can say on the surface that became different, but everything was different inside. There was no more a point of reference, what I used to identify myself with, which is this body, what I used to refer to as myself. That point of reference got shifted into awareness or consciousness. There was no longer anywhere or anything or anybody who was that person.

That's a tremendous change. Nothing was really different on the outside other than knowing everything was "me." There is nothing separate; everything is just here. Coming back to Satsang with Papaji after that, there was this recognition of coming home. Nothing is separate from that and just resting in that.

Some people have described similar experiences that don't last.

That has never changed. What changes is the outer experience. The blissfulness eventually passes. It's just another experience that arises in consciousness. But the simplicity and the clarity of resting as consciousness; that doesn't change.

I remember you saying in our last interview that your husband had a similar awakening, but it didn't last. I'm curious why it lasts for some and doesn't for others.

I would say there are different degrees of readiness for this recognition. What I found in my own experience is that there were many times I would taste this recognition, but I would still go back to the identification with the body. I spent hours sitting in bliss without anything moving inside, and yet the moment I would move out of that there would be suffering because there was still identification with this body.

It also depends on the karma or the destiny of the individual. There's nothing wrong with anything. Our perception is very small, our understanding of time is so limited, and we don't see the perspective of consciousness where everything is arising as it is. Everything is going where it's supposed to be going in its own time.

So there's nothing to "get."

Everything you "get" is going to go. If you want to get something, you can get it if you're lucky, and then eventually it will go, right? Yet there's this very pure desire for freedom that is really the movement and the motion of consciousness itself. Because consciousness, all it wants is to return back to its natural state, you see. That's the whole movement, that's what's happening. There's nothing else going on, so there's a very pure desire for that.

I'm touched by that [I have a few tears].

Just take a moment with that.

Yes, there's this kind of ache here in my heart... [We pause.] I like what you said about time... that the way we look at it is so limited. You used the words destiny and karma which we probably have a lot of misunderstanding around.

The way we understand time is based on this body. That's why it's limited because it's limited to its form, and that form is limited. That has nothing to do with consciousness, with reality. That is ongoing, and it has its own time and momentum and reason, its own motion.

Karma and destiny, there's much confusion and a lot of drama as well. All it means is that it's a momentum of things. Whatever has been set in motion needs to come to fruition. That's what it means in this realm of cause and effect because that's the only place karma exists. That's what destiny also means: whatever has been set in motion must come to fulfillment. If there has been a deep longing for freedom, if there has been good karma from the past... that is going to eventually come to fulfillment which is realization or enlightenment. It doesn't depend on anything or anybody. Once it is set in motion, there is nothing we can do about that. We can only be here.

Is there an individual soul? The way you describe it, it sounds like there is, though I know that's probably not true. Could you clarify what is setting this in motion?

It is complicated. I don't know if you want to include this.

That's what other people I have interviewed have said.

It's going to bring people into a lot of misunderstanding. Karma is not unique or personal to an individual. It's a certain stream of consciousness that carries a certain momentum. It's not individual-based. Yet in this reality here, it appears as a particular person who is going through certain things. But it's not personal. Consciousness does it all.

We can talk about the karma of an individual, the karma of a particular group of individuals, the karma of a country, a race—whatever gets set in motion by a certain movement in consciousness, that's what is going to have to come to fulfillment. All the time we are experiencing the results of that past. Most of the time, we believe those circumstances have something to do with something else. We don't realize it's a motion that's been set up in consciousness, and now it's coming to fulfillment which makes it really, really simple if we can see it like that.

I have this image. This particular body-mind has clothed or wrapped itself around some set of circumstances, an energy stream, but it's not personal. Is that accurate?

Yes. Once this motion is set in consciousness, it has to come to fulfillment. That means there's nothing we can do about the circumstances that arise. But we could *be here* just the way we are. In that *being here*, something stops. It doesn't go on anymore because that's what's going on in this karma field—constant perpetuation of suffering. Something gets set in motion, and sets something else in motion, "your" reactivity creates another involvement with that, and sets in motion something else. It goes on and on like that.

The tremendous power of Satsang is *being here*. The moment you are willing to be here, something stops. You are actually resting here as you are. Everything is attracted to that freedom, that space, because now there is some place to rest. It doesn't perpetuate. It comes and stops right here in that quiet willingness.

It's like there's space created when you stop. Openness attracts things to come in like a vacuum.

That's who you are. That's your nature, spaciousness. Once you're out of the illusion you're something else, everything can come and rest in that. Because that's what consciousness ultimately wants; it wants to rest here. Once that is available, anywhere in the universe, everything is going to come towards that because that's the place to end suffering. That's called Satsang.

Last night, one woman asked if there was a spiritual path you can suggest. You invited her to just be with what is. Is there any other ingredient other than this acceptance?

It's really tricky because there's nothing you can really do. Yet you can be honest about what arises in consciousness and take absolute total responsibility for what it is, no matter how much or how little you know about it. Let's say your recognition is very small, where you can vaguely taste that sense of freedom. Now you ask, "Am I willing to really embody that? Am I willing to follow that truth?" That's what I would call a willingness or a path, not to fall back to sleep, not to say, "Oh yeah, that was nice sitting in Satsang. Oh that was beautiful. Now let's just go back to the story." How about taking that truth and really allowing that to be your life, to be present in your life, to really take you out of that denial.

So being with whatever small or big awareness that comes up and being responsible to it.

Responsibility is such a charged word. Responsibility often means you're doing something wrong, and you have to do something better. You didn't take care. That's not how I mean it. I mean a total openness towards everything as it is, not denying that, not trying for anything to be different, not creating another story. To recognize that "as it is" is totally perfect, and you allow yourself to be here. Because our tendency is to blame, judge, move away from that to say, "Oh, it's happening because... he/she/him/them/it." The truth is that it's happening. Can I be here? That's what I call responsibility, being in response to what arises.

How did you get started teaching Satsang? But first, do you call yourself a teacher?

No. I don't refer to myself as anything. I started in 1995 or 1996. And how did I move into it? It arose in consciousness, this deep desire to share that with everybody. We can also say predestined; it was there to move in that way. It was very powerful. Once it started happening, at some point I realized, "Oh. Here I am sitting in Satsang and what about my guru, what about Papaji?" I remember having this conflict.

Then I had a dream Papaji came, and Ramana came, and we just walked together. Ramana said, "I have never seen such a sincere disciple." I realized I have to write to my guru and just ask him what he thinks about it. I wrote him a letter and told him there's this sharing happening since I came back, and said, "I only want to continue if you want me to continue because I don't want to do that without the sense that this is what you want also." He sent me a letter back and said, "Why do you want to give Satsang?" I sent an answer to him, and he sent a letter back and said, "OK."

I want to ask you about something you said last night about the top ten themes in Satsang.

Mostly what I see is a misidentification. That misidentification takes different forms. One of them is the story. There's a tendency to get involved with a particular story, we can call it personality. The involvement with a particular story will determine the different type of personality or the other way around. The basic core is the misidentification. Out of that, all these different stories arise.

There's a common theme of "not good enough," but what I become aware of as you speak is the one that I tend to identify with—the opposite, "being better than."

Yes, there's "I'm not good enough," and then there's "I am really good... I am better than anybody else," and any variation of those two themes. The bottom line is that there's a "not-OKness" in consciousness. Underneath all that is some unrest.

Part of the focus of the writing is about your individual, more personal life and how you are able to live in the world.

How to live this in the world... It's a tremendous experience to actually be here, to be available for everything that is happening and at the same time rest in that recognition; I consider it a blessing, actually. What I notice is there's a greater and greater willingness to align with what is true and really to rest in that. It's the willingness to bring all the parts of your experience, your life into that alignment.

So give us an example.

The voice of conditioning always has its own agenda about what needs to be done—not only *what* needs to be done but *how* it needs to be done. At the same time, there's an inner knowing of how things are, what could be happening, or how things could be taken care of. There's a willingness to come from what we know rather than from the conditioning itself because whenever we do that, the conditioning is going to create some trouble. We can only see things in a very limited perspective when we come from conditioning.

Same with relationship; we can enter relationship for different reasons. When you enter a relationship for the reason of truth and being, that's what is going to be the guiding force. Most of the time, we enter the relationship for other reasons—physical or emotional comfort or sexual attraction. We enter relationships for those reasons, we get entangled in it, and we don't understand why things are happening the way they're happening.

In relationship we have a lot of expectation and our conditioning very dramatically comes up because the relationship pressures you into looking at things. Conditioning always wants things to be a certain way. That's the limitation of it; that things can only work if they happen a certain way. What is needed is the willingness to align ourselves with what is true, really let go of expectation, and not follow the force of conditioning which arises so automatically. [She snaps her fingers.]

That's why I talk so much about willingness because you can start anywhere. It's the willingness to be here, to examine when conditioning is present, the willingness to see if it is really true or is it just coming from the past. The coming from the past is what creates suffering.

It seems like a relationship supports a kind of habitual behavior making it more challenging to be present.

Of course, and when I do talks on relationship, I say that all conditioning is going to arise in relationship—your past conditioning, his past conditioning. That's what we call the force of habit. We want certain things from each other and when that is not provided, we go into conflict or a power struggle. Yet it is possible to come from a different place, to come to rest in your self, to be really honest about what truly arises rather than what we think or want or who's right, who's wrong. The willingness to step out of that is powerful. Back into full responsibility: no one is out there doing anything to you.

How did you meet your partner, Life?

I met him maybe five years ago. He came to Satsang. It was obvious. There was this very strong pull to be together. It was so powerful that there wasn't anything that either he or I could do about that. It was very simple, very clear.

Do you feel like you entered in that relationship for the reason of truth and being?

Yes, but it doesn't mean that we don't have our dance, our habits, and it doesn't mean that we don't have ways that are habituated that come from the past and convenience. Yet there's tremendous willingness from both of us to talk very openly and honestly, to examine things, to just be here.

You and Life probably have conflict about something. Can you be specific about how it looks, what happens, how does it get resolved?

We are rarely in conflict, that's the first thing. When we are in conflict, it's because one of us has an idea about what needs to be done, one of us has an agenda. It becomes very apparent because that spaciousness of being that we usually experience in our relating is not available. So we become aware of that, and we are willing to point the other towards that as well. "Hey, sounds like something I have heard you say before many times... sounds like a story." [She laughs.] We are able to be very open and honest about it. There's an ongoing communication and investigation to look at things. The basic thing is we don't stay in the power struggle, not that we don't go there... we don't stay there. Neither one of us is willing to perpetuate that.

Is there something different about the way you see death now?

The interesting thing is that death happens all the time. We think it's this one-time event, and yes, there is a one-time event for this body. That's when the elements dissolve and come back to resting in whatever they are. They just dissolve at some point. I see it more as a transition, from one form, one state of being to another. Consciousness doesn't move, the physical elements just dissolve.

We are constantly faced with that everywhere. You look at nature; it's a constant cycle of creation and destruction, resting, and creation again. That's more my understanding of death right now and noticing that there is nothing here that is permanent. There is nothing you can hold onto. There's no place you can rest other than consciousness. It's an ongoing death and dying of any form or illusion or identity or understanding. There's nothing here really, no real permanence in anything.

You said last night that a teacher's role is to support your own Self-inquiry.

Yes, that's the role of the teacher, to stop that outgoing tendency, to let it rest in itself, its Source. That's why sometimes we meet a teacher externally who can actually speak the words of the inner teacher, the Self we all are. The Self speaks the words on the inside. Often we are not able to listen to that, so we need external form that would support and provide a level of inquiry until we are ready to rest in ourselves.

I know the message is really the same whether it's a male or female teacher, but there is a different flavor.

I don't know if it's different. What I see is consciousness teaching, not a teacher teaching; it's consciousness. It comes in a different form, different language, different conditioning, a different way it shares itself. Maybe for the sake of appearance, it's really helpful that it comes in the female body. There may also be a quality of tenderness which is more a mother kind of quality.

You use the word tenderness a lot in your teaching. Why is that so important?

Tenderness is important because there is so much self-judgment, criticism, and hardness in our conditioning. Often, even Self-inquiry can become a very judgmental place. What I find is that Self-inquiry requires discrimination which is very powerful and important. Without discrimination, we just go on with the story, but if discrimination is not grounded in tenderness, there is a danger of that becoming yet another place of self-loathing, judgment, and criticism.

That's what is coming forth right now in the world, the quality of the feminine, as you call it. Again, it has nothing to do with gender. It calls forth that tenderness, the allowing of everything to be here as it is, the real integration that is happening right now in consciousness. The purpose of teaching in this time is to bring everything to that real resting which is so grounded in being here. It seems like that's what the world needs right now; it needs to integrate in that way.

Is there anything more you would like to share?

If we can be here, everything is taken care of because that's who we are. Anything that supports you in resting, that's the most important right now. Being quiet, reading, sitting in Satsang, or doing service—whatever you do, if that's what supports you in being here. Everything else comes from that.

I know I am getting a little stuck in this idea that I have to have this kind of

awakening experience. In your ten years of teaching experience, I'm
wondering how you've seen this move in others.

Awakeness happens, that's for sure, there's no question about that. But you
don't have to teach awakening because it happens. There's nothing to be
done about that. That's why I always say that being here is so important
because you instantly transcend everything. The moment you can be here,
nothing else is necessary. You don't need to wake up, you don't need to be
enlightened, you don't need to be anything because you already *are.* [She
laughs.] It is very direct in that way.

If you are still chasing something, if you are still wanting awakening—
that means you're suffering. That means something is not OK just the way
it is, and just the way it is—which is perfect. Nothing has to be different.
Not before, not after, not ever. That's really the message, to let go of that
and just be here.

છ)લ્

When I walked outside, I found myself smiling for no good reason. I could
feel the perfection of it all. I drove home from the interview with the
windows down, singing one of my favorite Girl Scout songs. I found Chris
working in the garden. I joined him pulling weeds; no need to try and share
about the interview, just content to hum a tune and work side by side in the
bright sunshine.

છ)લ્

As the summer gave way to autumn, my contentment gradually faded. It
was Adyashanti's retreat in December that the familiar longing was stirred
awake. It was a physical ache in my chest whenever I took a moment to
contact the feeling. "What do you want?" Adya asked at the retreat. In a
small voice I said something about silence. He did not respond, and I knew

I wasn't being authentic. "It's deeper than that," I said. "It's hard to describe in words." "I thought it was deeper than that," he said. It was my fear of standing in front of a crowd that kept me from claiming in a clear, strong voice what I really wanted. "I want who I am. I want my Self."

He suggested I really feel what it's like to live with an ache in my heart, with that deep longing. "Be it," he said. "Don't just think about it. Let it lead you inside. No one else can do that for you." I followed his suggestion:

I am afraid to want, to really want something because in the past, my wanting led to disappointment. It started with wanting my Mom and Dad to stop drinking. I thought if they really loved me, they would listen to me. And when they didn't, I gave up. When you really want something, you open yourself to not getting it. And that's suffering. Better not to want anything too much—whether it's a more intimate relationship with Chris or a more intimate relationship with myself.

But the longing only kept growing stronger as the days grew shorter. It was uncomfortable and confusing. I started to focus the longing more and more on Chris and a desire for a deeper connection. I wanted Chris to read these interviews, to understand their words of wisdom, to share in a profound, deep way. That was not happening. Though he finally read the interviews, he refused to talk about them for fear I would not be happy with his response.

I finally scheduled a private session with Neelam to explore this because I was too much in the stew of it to see clearly. She gently guided me into my chest where the longing was the most obvious, and I let it have me. I cried and cried feeling the pain without resistance. Neelam asked me what it was like in my family growing up. It was the same pain then as now, wanting it to be different. As a child, it was my parents; now it is Chris. I felt this overwhelming sense of helplessness. That was at the core of the longing.

"Is helplessness OK?" she asked, "Not to *be* helpless but to *feel* helpless?" I let myself feel the helplessness, really feel the pain of wanting what I can't control. In that surrender arose a natural tenderness, an understanding and acceptance of myself.

Neelam explained that getting in touch with this soft, honest place is the foundation. From there, I can communicate what I want with Chris. First, I need to be totally honest with myself. I need to meet myself, and that means being willing to sit with the discomfort of helplessness and the not-knowing. I can't make someone love me just as it is not in my power to satisfy the longing for the truth of who I am. This helplessness can only be met with honesty and tenderness.

After that session, nothing outside me changed. But on the inside, something had shifted. One night I told Chris about this longing that has haunted me my whole life. I had no need for any particular response. I had no expectations he would even understand what I was talking about. I paused, and he reached out for my hand and gently kissed it. He looked in my eyes and said, "Oh Rita dear, I hope you find what you are looking for." I knew he was sincere.

In that moment, I saw him just as he is, someone doing the very best he can to love and support me. I smiled and thanked him for his love and understanding. It was as if the spell was broken. I was seeing the truth, and from that came contentment and acceptance. It set me free to turn my attention within, to the source of the longing, the wanting of who I am.

Catherine Ingram

Catherine, born in 1952 in Virginia, is the author of *In the Footsteps of Gandhi* (Parallax Press), *Passionate Presence* (Penguin Putnam) and a novel called *A Crack in Everything* (Diamond Books, 2006). Since 1992, she has led Dharma Dialogues and silent retreats and currently offers her work throughout the USA, Europe, and Australia. Formerly a journalist for 12 years, she specialized in issues of consciousness and activism and presently writes the *Life Advice* column for *Alternatives* journal in the Pacific Northwest. Catherine is also founder and president of Living Dharma, an educational non-profit foundation dedicated to principles of dharma in both silence and action.

CHAPTER 11

CATHERINE INGRAM

It was a release of madness or obsession with the story of my life,
my history, what was missing, what should be,
what might have been, all of those things.
It was a release of that internal demand
to make things better for myself.
And in its place was a deep appreciation for being alive
without asking for anything else.

I returned from Adya's retreat to find an email from Karen McPhee suggesting that Eckhart Tolle thought I should expand the book to include more well-known women. I thought I was done with the project since I had already packaged it up and sent it to the agent. I resisted at first, wondering if these women were "ordinary" enough. As I explored this question more deeply, I realized that this message would only be strengthened by including these women—the idea that regardless of appearances, we are all the same, both ordinary and extraordinary. I was learning this project had a life of its own, and I was in service to that, not the other way around.

I read Catherine Ingram's book *Passionate Presence* at the beginning, when the idea for the book first popped up. Her writing was simple and authentic. She seemed pretty "ordinary" even though she had written a book. I tried to contact her but when there was no response after a couple of attempts, I gave up.

This time when I tried to contact Catherine, her response was immediate. I guess it was the right timing. When I looked at her schedule for the next few months, I was delighted to see she was offering a weekend workshop in Hawaii. It seemed extravagant, but there was no better option to do the interview, and a break from the long winter on the mesa sounded delicious.

The minute I stepped off the plane in Maui, I was overwhelmed with the sweet fragrance and the warm, soft air. The palm trees swaying in the breeze seemed to be welcoming me back with open arms. It had been 12 years since I had last been to Hawaii where I lived for a couple of winters. I had forgotten how deeply nourishing it is to be in such a relaxing climate. The tension in my body I wasn't even aware of started to dissolve... the tightness that comes from the routine of winter—scraping icy windshields, driving on slippery roads, shoveling snow, and carrying wood. It's like letting out a big sigh and falling into the arms of a strong and loving mother.

I say "mother" because there is something so feminine about a tropical climate, so it was no surprise when I first met Catherine looking like a diva in a flowing skirt with a plumeria flower in her long brown hair. A group of about 30 had gathered to share Dharma Dialogues which is how Catherine refers to her *satsang*-type meetings. She greeted me warmly at the end of the evening before we began the silent retreat for the weekend.

As I drove back to where I was staying, I had to laugh at how silly it was to think Catherine could be anything but ordinary. It struck me that she was exactly my age and was a journalist before her life as a teacher. She had also experienced the death of a loved one (her brother) through AIDS.

The retreat was unlike any other—not much talking, not even what you would call meditation. Part of our afternoon included swimming in the ocean and walking along the beach, all in silence and with our senses wide awake. We sat together in the shade of a big tree overlooking the coastline, and Catherine invited us to gaze out at the world, taking it in with all our senses. My mind immediately resisted. "I traveled halfway around the world to just sit here and look at the ocean?!" Yes, that's exactly right.

I gradually slowed down and let myself receive the many sensations, the sights, the sounds, the smells. The beauty and perfection of each moment moved me to tears as I allowed myself to be fully present. This simple practice had a subtle effect of quieting my mind without any real effort. I felt deeply content.

The next day after the retreat, Catherine and I met at a busy restaurant in the little town of Paia to do the interview. We sat close together in a corner, passing the microphone back and forth so the background noise wouldn't interfere with the recording. It was like two friends talking over lunch. That's how it feels when you're with Catherine—she is both teacher and friend.

₧₨

As you look back to your childhood, what do you see as a kind of prediction about how you would be later in life?

I always felt I was going to escape from the place where I grew up which was rural Virginia. I felt different from pretty much everybody around me, and I somehow knew that place would not contain me for a minute longer than was necessary. I left when I was 18. I also had a sense from a pretty young age that I wanted to seek answers to the big questions. I had a horrible childhood, so I was forced to think about justice and fairness, whether life had meaning, and what's the point—all those kinds of questions.

By the time I was 12, I was obsessed with whether or not there was a God. I would watch a TV show that came on Friday nights at about 11:30 p.m. out of New York hosted by a guy named Joe Pyne. He was this iconoclastic character who would have all manner of weird people on his show. One night there was an agnostic on his show, and I decided at the age of 12 that's what I was. I was an agnostic.

I continued reading and seeking, and eventually my pursuits led me to Asian philosophies. I think I was 17 when I read *Be Here Now* by Ram Dass. I was profoundly affected by the book and decided I was going to read all of the books he recommended at the back of *Be Here Now*, which I did for the most part. I became steeped in both Buddhist and Hindu perspectives, still on this continual search.

But I didn't have any teachers, and in about 1973 I decided to go to India to find a guru. I went to Europe where I was making arrangements to go overland to India when I began hearing rumors about Naropa Institute which was going to open up in Boulder, Colorado in the summer of 1974. Naropa, founded by a Tibetan Rinpoche name Chogyam Trungpa, would be a new form of education, a dharma education. That opening summer, Naropa would host all kinds of famous teachers including Ram Dass. I was traveling alone, and it was hard being that young on the road. I didn't know what I was doing, really, so I decided it made sense to go back to my own country and attend Naropa Institute where many teachers would all be in one place, and I might have a hope of connecting with one of them.

There I met Ram Dass and attended all his talks. I also met Joseph Goldstein and was very influenced by his course called "Essential Buddhism." I was taken by the simplicity of the Buddhist teachings and by Joseph's presentation of them, so I started doing retreats with Joseph and his colleagues. I became more and more involved with that scene and became a manager and an organizer. In 1976 I helped found the first US center in that tradition in Massachusetts called Insight Meditation Society, which is still going strong and about to have its 30th anniversary. Buddhist study and Buddhist practice became my way of life at that time. All my friends were Buddhist. It was a world unto itself, a budding movement that in those early days was not the mainstream thing that it is now. It was fairly esoteric, really. Meditation was something that was extremely uncommon.

What were the limitations for you of that approach?

After many, many years of practice, I found myself feeling somewhat dry. OK, I could watch my mental landscape fairly well, but there was a kind of "so what." I didn't feel much joy or particularly connected in a kind of juicy sense to this reality, to this existence. There was a lot of emphasis on detachment at that time in that tradition. I always yearned for much more of a heart connection, a more full-bodied way of being. I didn't really have a perspective to get me there until I met Poonjaji in 1990. Before that, I became disillusioned and fell into a deep depression.

You say depression. How did that look for you?

It was a kind of existential gloom—feeling everything is pointless... chasing experiences, relationships, power, and money is just crazy. You're never going to get happy that way. Then because my dharma connection had more or less fallen away, I didn't have anything to turn to there either. I felt like a stranger in a strange land, like I didn't belong here. I could hardly get myself to the grocery store. I would go there and see these people who were living a sort of normal life, having conversations, just chatting, a couple deciding what kind of pancake mix to get. I would look at them and marvel that people were living in ordinary realities and content in them, or relatively so anyway. It was not within my reach. I'd seen through. I'd opened some horrible veil and peered into this shocking, meaningless void.

How did you know what to do? What arose?

I was, of course, very open to a new perspective. When you're in that state, you're extremely open to any new perspective. A few of my friends started coming back from seeing Poonjaji, and they were very transformed. One of my girlfriends who was a Vipassana teacher came back from a trip to see him and tried to describe it to me. I said, "Well, what does he actually teach?" She laughed and said, "All I can tell you is that we would stand outside at night and laugh at the moon."

When she said that, some bright burst happened inside of me, and I thought to myself, "God, I would like to stand outside and laugh at the moon. I would really like to do that." Something called me in that moment. Gangaji and I were long-time friends, and she also contacted me when she got back from Poonjaji and said, "You really should go and meet him." It was about a year before I actually managed to get there even though these friends were very persuasive and were returning obviously transformed.

I was in a relationship and having a grand old time, but still this existential undercurrent was there. Then my relationship ended. It actually ended several times. After the first big breakup, I went straight to Poonjaji. I was broken-hearted and back in my big existential mired morass. I interviewed Poonjaji on an assignment with *Yoga Journal*, an old journalistic trick to be able to spend time with whomever I wanted. [We smiled in acknowledgement of this common bond.] I got six hours one on one with him in the first week of my being there in addition to the public *satsang*.

In that week, I became a different person than the one who had arrived in Lucknow—than the person I'd been my whole life. I was very, very changed. It was a release not an addition. It was a release of madness or obsession with the story of my life, my history, what was missing, what should be, what might have been, all of those things. It was a release of that internal demand to make things better for myself. And in its place was a deep appreciation for being alive without asking for anything else. That produced a sense of freedom. People think freedom is going to be some esoteric, unusual thing that descends on you in some magical way when, in fact, it is only the letting go of the apparent bondage.

You use the word "freedom." Is that the same as "awakening"?

The word "awakening" is often used in a synonymous way with this feeling of freedom that can occur in a moment in time. The irony is when it does occur, you realize there was nothing really blocking it in the first place. It's a strange paradox. Poonjaji used to say you will laugh when you see this because you'll realize, "Oh, there were no chains on me all this time. It was all imagination." At that point you also realize you know this feeling. You just weren't quite honoring it as such. Then you begin to honor it and really let your awareness float there much more frequently once you grok there's nothing more to do. There's no attainment. None at all.

You hear this, the Zen masters say it, everybody says it, but people don't quite believe it. When they hear the word "awakening," people sometimes imagine a huge event that's going to add on all kinds of new information. But that is not, in my experience, what happens. What happens is the previous fixation on one's made-up story is no longer interesting, and then freedom or the clear awareness is just shining through in its own natural way.

I have heard about a whole range of experiences where some people have this big moment, sort of an "ah ha," and some people are much more gradual in this process.

The Zen perspective covers this very well, the ideas of sudden and gradual awakening. In a way you could say both are so. There can be an ah-ha where you see there was never any bondage, the idea of a gateless gate. You thought you went through a gate, but looking back you see there was no gate in the first place. Or you realize this sense of freedom, and it's actually very familiar. In those moments you can say there's sudden recognition. However, there's a gradual getting used to it, and there's a gradual permeation of it throughout the life. There's a steeping in your own self, in your own relaxation in this, and that gets stronger. It informs all of your relationships and your work.

All of this comes in the steeping, which I speak about it in my book, *Passionate Presence: Seven Qualities of Awakened Awareness*. We don't try to attain or look for those qualities, but they arise on their own when we are in relaxed present awareness. Discernment comes. Embodiment arises knowing that you are embedded here in this earth on which you depend to sustain your life. There's tenderness, the sweetness and poignancy of feeling for others. Silence, a quietness in the heart. A sense of wonder, where you understand you are living in a grand mystery, and you no longer try to make up stories and myths about it or believe any of the ones that are around. You begin to realize you don't need to have a fairy tale to live, and in fact, it's a form of maturity to stand in wonder and realize, "I don't know."

After your visit with Papaji, did you ever return to any sense of separation or depression?

When I met him, there was a huge transformative letting go of the gnarly, habitual story I had known since childhood. But I had many, many dips into sadness, neurosis, and moroseness subsequent to meeting Papaji, and I even had a long period of grief at the final ending of the relationship I spoke of before. But all of those difficult feelings and mind states were happening in a much bigger space. They happened like a thunderstorm in an open sky. It didn't matter as much that there were these phases and these feelings and moments of depression and so on. I realized, "Oh, this is another aspect of freedom." Freedom can handle some waves of suffering. It can handle a lot of suffering. Now I just let the feelings be because I don't feel myself shrink-wrapped around any particular set of feelings. I feel myself as expansive.

Did you have the childhood dream you would grow up, get married, and have children?

I was a romance addict as a child, and I actually think my own particular dharma taste tends to be very engaged with passion. I'm more of a Sufi than I ever was a Buddhist. I had a real fixation on romance as a child. I was very dreamy. I'm sure I was using it partially as an escape from the torments of my childhood conditioning. Yes, I suppose I thought I would get married, but I never saw myself having a conventional life.

I always saw something very exotic and glamorous. As a young teen I used to read Auntie Mame books. She was this wild fictional character who traveled the world and was always arriving from Fiji or Bhutan or somewhere equally strange and sweeping everyone off their feet with new adventures.

It sounds a little bit like your life now.

Yes, I think I was very much influenced by Auntie Mame, and that's certainly how my nephews and nieces see me.

When you came back from India, how did you get started teaching?

I had lunch with Ram Dass in San Francisco one day in 1992, and I was telling him about my experience in India with Poonjaji when out of the blue he said "Would you come and teach with me at my retreat at Omega Institute?" I just burst out laughing and said, "Teach what?" And he said, "Just speak exactly like you've spoken at lunch. Just talk about your experience." I thought, "Well, I could do that maybe." I went to his retreat and because he drew hundreds of people, my first teaching experience was with a large crowd of people at an afternoon workshop. It was fun, and I really enjoyed it.

After all those years of dharma life on the road and with so many friends rapping about our experiences all the time, I had a certain facility for talking about these things. Ram Dass invited me to do a few more of those with him, and people started to invite me to come to their cities. That's how I began more or less on my own. I can tell you, it had never occurred to me before that to teach. It had never crossed my mind until Ram Dass asked me, and for that I'm very grateful.

You didn't change your name. Was that ever a question for you?

I never had the slightest interest in getting a different name. I never saw the point. I don't understand why one would add on to identification. [She laughs.] Of course, some people's teachers gave them a name to perhaps identify themselves in a different way from a habitual pattern. For myself, I never had any attraction to that.

I remember you talking at the retreat about not wanting to align yourself with Buddhism or Advaita.

As time has gone on, I haven't wanted to be affiliated with any religious perspective, tradition, or system primarily because I see the ways those ideas catch people and limit them. I always say, "Take the best and leave the rest." Take whatever it is from any of those traditions. When you hear it, you know it already in your heart, and you can celebrate there's something you yourself know but perhaps had not articulated in that way. If something doesn't resonate, leave it. Don't try to contort yourself into some mold even if some of what you are hearing makes sense.

That's unfortunately what I see a lot of people doing and what I did as a practicing Buddhist. Because I loved so much of the Buddhist perspective, I kept trying to make myself fit with all of it. I kept trying to have an experience of no-Self or of emptiness, for example. For years and years, I tried to fit myself into a mold of experiencing emptiness when, in fact, what I was experiencing was fullness.

It turns out if you take a given amount of space and remove all particles from it, elementary particles will arise out of that emptiness, out of apparent nothingness. On a purely physical reality, there's no such thing as emptiness. I kept trying to find something I would now say is impossible to find.

I hear these kinds of mistaken assumptions and contortions in so many questions. I hear it constantly. I feel that in Dharma Dialogues I am mostly just debunking spiritual myths and belief systems.

What is the greatest misunderstanding you hear when you're giving Dharma Dialogues?

The greatest one is that there's some reason for a search.

And why is there no reason for a search?

Because nothing is lost, the greatest joke of the whole spiritual journey. There's no reason for a search at all. As Poonjaji said, "Call off the search." When I met Poonjaji, all searching fell away. The seeking absolutely stopped. It's not as if I landed in some kind of perfection or enlightenment, not at all. It's that the folly of trying to change this—working on the "me" project, trying to purify my mind, trying to realize something, having a spiritual perspective—all of that fell away into this great appreciation for my life, my conditioned mind, my reality exactly as it is.

When you see you don't have to mess with the program at all, when you let it be exactly as it is, and you realize you're able to suffer when it happens, grieve when it happens, and laugh joyously when it happens— all of it coming and going in this great expanse of existence—then you really are home free. You don't need any stories or denial of what you are. You don't have to have a buffer or strategy of beliefs between you and reality.

Tell us more about the way you invited us to be the "awake animal."

It's an emphasis that has been coming more strongly in the last few years of sharing. I speak a lot about how when we are attuned in this way, more and more we experience ourselves as an awake animal, a human animal immersed in and fully experiencing its senses. You see, you smell, you taste, and you feel. You're less obsessed with thoughts.

Most people are entranced in thought, and they're barely sensing themselves as creatures. I think that's where a lot of the problem is on this planet. We have lost touch with nature; with the ecology out of which we are born and are dependent our whole lives. This understanding puts you directly in touch with this embodied animal form.

In my experience on the beach, there was this fear of being too open. You asked, "Can you bear it, the beauty and the pain of life?" Really, do we have a choice?

Once this opening starts happening on its own, you no longer have much choice. It just keeps going. As Nisargadatta said, "It's like a spark in a shipload of cotton." It's inevitably burning the dross. One becomes more and more sensitive while the burning may become even more intense. You might even sometimes wish you could go back, but not really, because going back only means the armoring, the closing down and distancing.

Just as the obsession with neurotic thought is a habit, there can be the habit of freedom. When you recognize freedom would be preferable, you let awareness drift or float there more often. You start to prefer that taste, and the habit becomes stronger. It's a very organic process. You're spending more time in the floating, free clear awareness as an awake sensing animal, and you spend less time indulging the crazy stories. Even though they arise, you don't care. They don't interest you.

You said something about how it is just a shift in attention. Instead of focusing on the thoughts, they're still there, but they're in the background instead of the foreground.

Exactly correct. They become background like whispers that are constantly dissolving and are not really a problem any longer. I keep emphasizing that you lose interest in the neurotic material. That's a really important thing. The only reason those thoughts are taking up the screen of your awareness is because there's an interest in the story. When you lose interest, which is quite possible to do in this habit of freedom when those thoughts come, there is no movement of attention toward them. You lose interest in what's not real. So much suffering of mind is imaginary. You start to lose interest in imaginary suffering.

Someone in the retreat said that many of his thoughts are there to entertain. We talked about how this culture is over-stimulating for us, how it's never enough.

It has to do with one of my other favorite subjects, contentment. I see contentment as the radical political stance of our time—what is required to reverse this juggernaut of more, more, more. More experience, more stuff. Teenagers now are simultaneously doing instant messaging on their computers, surfing the web, listening to music on their headsets, watching a movie on their flat screen, and talking on the phone. It's a barrage of stimulation that I think is very harmful to the nervous system. It's making people crazy, and that's why we have a drugged-out culture, starting with the kids. Unfortunately, America is exporting this around the world, and I see no good coming from it on any level. There's greater violence, rape of the resources of the planet, pollution, we're running out of oil, on and on it goes. It's kind of a horror.

Contentment stops it in its tracks. If you are grooving on the simplicity of watching a sunset and sharing a meal with your loved ones, there's not much the advertising media can really tempt you with. You can actually enjoy your precious life and the precious moments that are left to you.

I'm reminded of my husband who died 12 years ago who said near the end of his life, "Who I am is enough." It's a touchstone for me, and it has greater and deeper meaning as time goes on.

What a gift for you to have known those words in this way. My brother struggled with life so much, but once he got the diagnosis with AIDS, he started really living. He knew his days were numbered, and he really lived those last years despite the fact that there was a lot of physical pain.

How do you see death, and how has it influenced you?

Because I don't have many beliefs, or I try not to have any beliefs although they creep in now and again, I don't have any idea about what if anything happens after death. I have no sense that my brother who died in 2002 is somewhere or that I will ever have any reunion with him. I don't have any sense of continuation or remembrance of previous lives either.

So for me, this life is the one I am interested in, and the only one I can say I actually know is real. What has been of comfort to me with regard to death is that rather than the identification with this Catherine creature whose time does seem limited, my identification moves out into what you could call the primordial force that flows through all which is constantly blossoming and dying. When I identify with that force as my great ancestor, there's a sense of continuity. Not personal, but impersonal continuity and that gives some comfort. As for this personal reality, I don't have any sense of anything beyond this.

At the retreat, you talked about what happens when we die, what's left.

What's left is the love we shared. That's pretty much all that's left of our essence, the love that's living in the heart of those who loved you, whose lives you touched. At some point, they will be gone, and the love just floats around impersonally. It's like a flame that gets passed on and on. Beyond that, one can leave works of art, some writings, a monument, or something like that, but that's not much of your essence, not in the way the love you shared lives in someone's being.

You said you don't have many beliefs. Can you talk about the distinction between direct experience and beliefs.

Beliefs are things people have read, heard, or have been taught but have no direct knowledge of in their experience, in their own lives. The importance of recognizing and living by this distinction is that people are no longer operating from untruths, myths, and stories. People are operating from the truth.

What is happening on this planet with regard to religion and religious belief is a horror, everywhere you look. Much of religious belief, even New Age and Eastern ones, are very repressive. They shut down life in various ways. In Dharma Dialogues I am constantly challenging people's myths as I see how limiting those myths are in their lives, even the best ones, even the intelligent ones.

Why is it we're so drawn to some of these beliefs, like the concept of reincarnation or the idea that the soul is doing this progressive journey?

People want eternity, "me" forever.

Oh, that's it! [We laugh.]

That's the carrot religions have sold. Otherwise people would flee from religion as fast as you could move your legs. If you're going to get the upgrade into heaven, and all you have to do is shut down your life here for this temporal amount of time and space, trade it for paradise or nirvana or whatever your belief system happens to be—people want to make that deal although they usually fail. They can't bear to do all the religious rules even with the promise of an eternity of happiness.

I remember one of my friends who was reared in a strict Catholic home believed kissing a girl before marriage was a mortal sin. He told me at 14, he French-kissed a girl, and he decided at that moment he was going to spend the rest of eternity in hell because he wasn't about to give up kissing. [She laughs.]

Some people do give it up and shut down all the natural joys and instincts. All they think about is some sort of escape from reality. You see the madness it causes, the anger, the repression of sexual instincts that causes perversions of all sorts. We can thank religion for all of this. We can also thank religion for the anti-homosexuality beliefs. It's not unnatural in nature itself. Nature produces ten per cent homosexuals in all primates. It's totally a manmade idea that homosexuality is not OK or that it is not natural.

Speaking of myths, what about the idea that you create your own reality. This seems to be a big one.

I like how Ken Wilber said it, that only psychotics create their own reality. Of course, there is a place for intentionality and action based on thought and planning. A mature person understands they're not really in control of how things turn out, even with the best laid plans. So you make the plans with a light awareness, and plans may or may not come to be. You don't have a sense you're actually creating a great swath of reality.

In some Advaita circles there's a sense of no "doer." It's all grace, and you just sit back and wait for something to happen. How do you respond to that idea?

We can argue until the cows come home about free will and destiny, and I don't think anybody knows. I always say if choice is appearing, then choose freedom. What we can see in our own direct experience is that we have intentionality. That's how you got to Hawaii where we are having this conversation. That's how I managed to get here as well... a lot of intention and planning.

So these are very basic, practical things. I like things on the ground. I am not interested in philosophical debates. When I speak about intentionality for freedom, it is a light, easy intention, non-striving, effortless intention—just a turning toward the light, like a plant. The plant isn't saying, "Now I am going to turn towards the sun." There is some innate intentionality turning towards the light. We can have that sense about our own lives, if your life happens to be graced with this interest and is turning more towards that.

I'd like to talk about how the feminine is contributing to what's happening in the world today.

I love the perspective of the feminine force. If we are going to be saved as a species, and I'm not clear that we will be but if we are, it will be because a feminine perspective becomes predominant and men will have to embrace this perspective. The march of force, destruction, and violence that's going on is so out of balance. The feminine perspective is family, harmony, interdependence, and communication. It is relational and is saying, "It's just *us* here, we're all family, let's take care of each other, let's be kind, let's embrace instead of fight."

This kind of dharma perspective comes with the quieting of the heart we have been talking about all weekend. One of the natural qualities is tenderness. I think the masculine force is terrified of tenderness. It shuts it out; it's too much feeling. We're going to have to get into feeling together if we're going to save this particular species and the many others who are going down because of us.

This resistance to feeling reminds me of my own attempts to see emptiness which I now see as a more patriarchal view. I see a lot of those transcendent views as patriarchal. This world is nothing. This is an illusion. Let's transcend into the outer limits, into space, into nothingness, into mind only. But no, that's not working and hasn't ever worked. [She laughs.] The only divinity we know is right here in this body and this earth.

What do you see happening from your perspective traveling all over the world?

It's almost as if there's an intensification of the forces of darkness and light, an intensification of polarization. The extreme detour our country has taken away from the most beautiful values in these last years under this embarrassing, destructive administration, and people in power, and the apathy among the opposition to the people in power to combat it; this has actually quickened the light in other places. Lots of other places don't want to be like us. Governments that probably would not have been voted in—liberal, progressive, socialist governments—are being elected in reaction to this darkness that's going on in the United States. It's really an interesting time, and who knows how it's going to play out. Polarities do tend to intensify each other. As one gets stronger, the other also gets more intense as well.

What's our role in this time?

Someone asked me at the end of the retreat, "Isn't it important to have responsibility?" I said, "It's very important to have response-ability. To be able to respond clearly, one needs to be in one's right's mind and heart." This very perspective I am speaking about is the best way to be in your right mind and heart and be able to discern what is needed and what is the best way to effect that need. You can have great intentions, but if you're not very clear and not very loving in your heart, your actions may just become part of the problem. There are many, many cases of that.

It is important to place freedom first and no longer be a body on the pile of the problem but get into your wholeness, into your own joy, into your own clear seeing then offer the spilling of the well of your being. It's a spillover of goodness. It may not change the tide, but at least it won't be harmful. And it may, in fact, change the tide as we've also seen in history.

You said something about not being attached to the outcome.

You have to give it all over. Whether we're going into Armageddon or a golden era of greater consciousness on this planet, our work is the exact same. It's the same each day. We let our own neurosis fade into the background of awareness. We stay instead with the embodied, awake animal, the sensation of being. That automatically brings with it a feeling of being connected to the earth and to its living forms. It brings tenderness, sweetness, kindness towards others, natural ethics, discernment about how to behave and wonder, all the things that enable us to live in a gentle way here on this earth. Whatever happens, we will have lived in harmony for these brief moments we are here.

ഇറ്റ

After our interview, I stayed in Hawaii for another week, and I was able to really practice what I had learned at the retreat. Whenever I would get lost in thought, I remembered to return to my senses. I would wake up to what was happening around me—the birds singing, the sound of the surf, the warm breeze on my skin. This was pretty easy to do while on vacation surrounded by beauty. But even in "paradise," the mind found plenty of problems to chew on. It was actually pretty funny when I took a step back and watched the show. I didn't take it too seriously. I simply noticed I was off on a tangent again, and I would gently bring my attention back to what was here now, the sights, and smells, and sounds of this moment.

This was harder to do when I came home. My morning walk on the mesa was a good time to practice because though I was surrounded by beauty and the sights and sounds of nature, I was not on vacation. I was getting ready for my day at work which would lead my mind into all manner of preparations—planning the phone calls I needed to make, making a list of errands when in town, deciding on what outfit to wear that day, familiar habits. Even when I was more or less aware what was happening, I would sometimes return from my walk and realize I didn't remember much about it—the color of the sky, the smell of the air, whether there were any birds singing. I was simply not present, and that seemed like a real loss. I was missing out on this one precious life!

Life takes vigilance, I realized. It is not just relaxing into the moment. It is also about waking up in the moment and noticing what is really happening. Am I present or am I in a story? Catherine had given me a simple and very effective way to stay present: bring your attention to the senses. Be an awake animal. Let the story fade in the background.

Gangaji

Gangaji, born in 1942 as Toni Roberson, grew up in Mississippi. Gangaji was asked by Papaji to give *satsang* in 1990 and has since traveled all over the world offering her invitation to peace and fulfillment. She is the author of *The Diamond in Your Pocket: Discovering Your True Radiance*, *You Are THAT!* Vol. I and II and *Freedom and Resolve: The Living Edge of Surrender*. She recently moved to Ashland, Oregon where she lives with her partner of 30 years, Eli Jaxon-Bear.

CHAPTER 12

GANGAJI

This is the secret I really have to offer—
that we all can just be people,
and this is more extraordinary than any of us can know.
There is something huge in just being truly human.

When I first thought about including Gangaji, I was too intimidated to ask her. I thought she would be too busy or famous to have time for this project, making the assumption that it would not be important enough to someone so important. But once again, life had another idea. The very last day I was in Hawaii, I went on a whale watch with a good friend who introduced me to a woman who had worked with Gangaji for nine years. She encouraged me to include Gangaji and gave me a person in her office to contact. When I got home, that's what I did. I was met with a warm welcome and an invitation to attend two small, intimate *satsang* gatherings—a contrast to the more typical two to three hundred people that Gangaji usually attracts. A few weeks later, I was on a plane to Ashland, Oregon.

Many of those in attendance had been meeting with Gangaji for a while and she knew just what they needed—sometimes a challenge, sometimes support. To one person, she threw the beanbag signaling that he was in some kind of a story. To another, she tossed a rose to acknowledge her beauty and put an end to her self-criticism. There was a way that Gangaji was warm and loving, but also sharp and challenging.

Someone asked about how we can make ourselves more available to silence. Gangaji paused and said, "It is the way we make ourselves *unavailable* to silence that we can bring our attention to. Silence is stillness and stillness is death and it is natural to avoid it." She invited us to stop the strategizing, the controlling and the distractions and meet death fully.

Then another man talked about how he had found comfort in becoming a Christian. "That's fine that you have invited Jesus into your heart," said Gangaji, "but don't make it one way." She invited him to meet Jesus, to go into his heart, climb up there onto the cross with him. "What a story," Gangaji went on to say. It's a story of complete failure, of utter despair. Here's this man who comes with a message, a beautiful message and no one can hear it. His followers leave him. He was even abandoned by God. Why? Because we have to find it out for ourselves, without being taken care of by a "Father," by the "other."

Let yourself be crucified, she said. Meet the despair. Meet the utter hopelessness that you will ever figure this out. This form, this individual "me" can never hold the silence, the formless. That's what dies. And then there is redemption. And only then is there a full life.

The man she was talking to shook his head and wondered out loud why he had come to hear this depressing message. Gangaji smiled and reminded him of what he already knew—that the comfort that his belief in Christianity provided was not enough for him. It's enough for some, she said gently, but not enough for you, is it?

The room was completely silent. Gangaji was silent, too. Then she thanked the man for his deep and honest sharing and left the room, touching my shoulder lightly as she walked by. I couldn't move. I sat there for a long time as people quietly started to leave the room. I began to write in my journal:

So what if it really is over right now? Can I go there? No more chance of making the relationship work or getting enlightened or finding happiness. Oh no. A part of me screams, "I want to get it." And I am calling for help to something outside of me, some big mama or daddy to pick me up and take care of me, hold me like a baby. That's the feeling, like I am throwing a tantrum. "I want it! And I want you to give it to me."

Oh Father, why hast thou forsaken me? That line from the Bible cuts right to the heart of it. That's how I feel, even though I don't even believe in a God like that! It is programmed in me to want to be saved somehow. But in the end, I know I am on my own. There is no one to hold me, no one to be held. No other. I am the one.

I feel this longing so strongly for my life to mean something. I want to share my message, my gifts. I don't want to die. I see now that the crucifixion is about letting this "me" die—my life, my message, my gifts. The "me" can't have what I am longing for. The me isn't big enough. Life is bigger than this little me.

I walked slowly back to where I was staying at a good friend's house. The fruit trees were completely covered in pink blossoms, the tulips and daffodils were dancing in the breeze, it was a bright spring day. I breathed in the warm air, grateful to be alive.

The following day, I met Gangaji at her home in the late afternoon. Her house was at the end of a short lane set back from the street. She was just saying goodbye to one of her assistants on the front porch when I walked up. She greeted me with a warm hug and invited me in. We wandered to the back deck, which overlooked a grassy meadow and a small stream lined with tall green trees. It was a peaceful scene but we decided to do the interview indoors in a cozy corner of the living room where it was quieter.

I thought I would be more nervous. This is someone famous, my mind warned, as if it was afraid that I might do something stupid. So I took special care to make sure the equipment was working. But as soon as the tape recorder started rolling, I relaxed and the questions flowed easily. Sometimes I would see Toni (her former name) in her facial expressions and sometimes there was the more impersonal gaze of a wise woman. Once or twice I forgot about the questions as I gazed into her still eyes. Her presence alone was the answer to any question I had.

ഊഗ

I'd like to start off with a little bit about your story, about how some of your life events can be seen as a kind of thread leading to where you are today.

I relate to the book's title about ordinary women, because I consider myself ordinary, but I also know there is no such thing as ordinary, and this is truly extraordinary. As ordinary people, we think that extraordinary is "out there." Famous or revered people's lives get turned into myths.

There is a way I could speak of my life as regular and mundane, but the truth is, like all individual lives, there has been a particular thread throughout. That thread is the recognition, "I am," a recognition that consciousness is here, and a kind of thrill at that.

At around five or six years old, I struggled to find some way to express this recognition, and for me, initially, it was to fall in love with Christ. To the horror of my parents, I fell passionately, ecstatically, in love with Jesus in Sunday school. I built shrines around the house to the Virgin Mary until my father said that we didn't do those things. So, I got the message: "We don't do that. That is 'over the top.'"

After receiving this message, my life became a question of how to be both normal and happy. I perceived myself as not being normal. Ordinary, yes, but not normal. I attempted to pursue what was considered normal. I sought happiness through popularity, through being an exceptional student, through marrying the right man and having a child. My husband was a great father and a real gentleman. He loved me, yet I was still unhappy because, obviously, these are not the right reasons to marry. Real love and connection were overlooked because it was all about "me." Looking back now, I can only say that it was a life of trivial pursuits.

When marriage didn't bring happiness, I divorced and began searching for it through other avenues—sexuality, drugs, spirituality—always sensing that there was something alive inside that was extraordinary. I figured that if it wasn't coming out, I was doing something wrong. My life became a search to correct "me."

There was always something missing, and I felt that either there was something wrong with me, or there was something wrong with the people I was with. [She laughs]. Either way, it was clear that something was wrong.

When I left my husband, it felt wrong to leave such a good situation, but I also thought something was wrong with him, and that I didn't love him in the passionate way that I needed love. This was in San Francisco in the early 70s, so I was in the right place at the right time to act out the passion of those years.

After leaving my husband, I was falling apart, so I went to see a typical Freudian psychoanalyst. I saw him five times, and he helped me tremendously. It was at this time that I discovered a sense of ugliness inside myself, an unlovable inner monster. The therapist was quite helpful in supporting my examination of this horror. I give credit to basic Western psychoanalysis for helping me shift my attention within, which eventually led me toward a spiritual search.

In 1976, I met my second husband, Eli, and recognized him as my teacher. He was much deeper on the spiritual path than I was. I saw that he knew something I didn't know. Plus, I simply knew that he was the one.

Eli had been living in a commune in Oregon. At first he seemed like a sweet kid in overalls—I'm five years older than he. But then I fell in love with him. He was very serious about his spiritual search, and I saw that if I was going to be with him, I had to be serious too!

What was your own search about at the time?

I had tasted many paths. There were many gurus coming through town, although at that time I couldn't really relate to the whole guru scene. I was still waiting to see what was out there that was right for me.

What was it about the gurus that you couldn't get into?

The guru subculture didn't attract me at all. It seemed like a regression. Yet

I saw that the people involved were taken by something, so I assumed I was somehow missing the essence of it. I would sit with a guru, and go through the devotional motions, but nothing sparked inside me. I couldn't stay with it because for me it was drudgery. You had to get up at 5:00 a.m., meditate and chant, and eat food that tasted horrible.

Eli became my focus as a teacher because he was involved in Taoism and t'ai chi. Once I started reading Lao Tsu, I began to be drawn to something within that was very deep and very still. I also wanted to see the way Eli wanted me to see so that he would be attracted to me. That's the truth of the matter.

Whatever works! [We laugh.]

However the true search catches you, it catches you. That time was beautiful. I started reading the *I Ching* and *The Secret of the Golden Flower*. By then, we had moved to Bolinas where the atmosphere was different from San Francisco. The focus was nature rather than the stimulation of the city. This was the late 70s, and in Bolinas, I began to study massage therapy.

At that point, my love for Eli was what was really penetrating me, and a level of surrender that I had never before experienced. I had always been the one in charge in relationships. He wasn't even interested in a monogamous relationship or a life partner, so I had to face a lot of jealousy.

Eventually, he fell in love with me, and we did become partners, but the first phase was a trial of fire, and I had to trust myself that this was a sane relationship because it appeared insane. He was young, and he still had issues to work out around his mother and other women. I could see this, and I wondered if I wasn't supremely stupid to fall for him. Finally, I just had to trust myself, and this in itself was a great teaching.

Relationship has always been my teacher, going as far back as my grandmother. She was, for me, a spiritual teacher, a teacher of love and fun. When I eventually met my final teacher, Papaji, he was also relational. He wasn't impersonal. His was a true "hello," not just to the life that was in me, but also to me as a person.

During those first five years with Eli, I attended a college of acupuncture in England. I liked the Eastern philosophy of healing, and I wanted to make a living at something more than massage therapy. We started living a different kind of life after that, a more material life. We moved to Mill Valley and opened a clinic in San Francisco. Eli was offering hypnotherapy and NLP, and I had an acupuncture practice. We lost some of the sweet, easy, natural life we had in Bolinas, but I can see now that this was necessary.

It was around that time that we discovered the Enneagram, which was a major discovery for us both. Through understanding what the fixation was for this particular mind/body, I also began to see how much of my story of suffering was self-created. It was also the time of New Age ideas such as how to create your own reality. I stopped being a victim and became a liberated, feminist woman.

It was a good life, yet there was something still missing. Here I was, happy with my mate, living a successful life in the world, getting great feedback as a healer, looking good, and earning enough money to have a house in Mill Valley. Living in the Bay Area felt like living in the center of the world.

Still, there was a core of suffering. I knew that somehow this life was not living its full potential. There was an underlying energy. Not so much a story, but more like a depression. It was a sense of weight in my heart.

When Eli and I were going through a great period in our relationship, or there were beautiful moments in nature or meditation, this feeling would diminish, but it was always waiting for me, haunting me. I wasn't indulging it like I had been, but it was still there in the room.

Eli also experienced something unfulfilled within him. We had succeeded at so many different things, yet there was something unfinished and we both knew it. That's when we both knew that we needed a teacher. Though we had been with many of the teachers who passed through our area, and felt a connection with some, none of these connections stayed with us. We found ourselves praying for a teacher.

We recognized that our life in Mill Valley was draining us. It was the late 80s and we were living the high life, working hard, eating out all the time, and worrying about the mortgage. We decided to sell our house and move to Maui where I had once lived. We intended to open a center on Maui, and we found a place we could buy if we sold our house. We made the move and were in negotiations for the new center when someone came in with cash and snatched it up. We were crushed at the time, but of course, it was perfect in the end. So here we were on Maui, surrounded once again by nature, drinking it in, loving it, and wondering, "What now?"

We continued to pray for a teacher. I went back to the mainland and heard Andrew Cohen speak, one of the first Western teachers to come from Papaji. I got Eli to come hear Andrew as well, and we recognized that this Westerner was not speaking in traditional Eastern terminology. He was simply speaking the truth to people directly, and it was startling.

It was Eli who eventually found Papaji, though he wasn't looking for him specifically. He was looking for some Tibetans and Sufis who he'd had a connection with. He was looking for someone deeply awake, and this led him to Papaji. He wrote me and said, "This is it, it's here, it's alive, it's real; you have to come." This was 1990.

After all these years of searching, how did you avoid getting cynical, or giving up and resigning yourself to a more mundane life?

I have no idea, really. I would have to call it grace. It was very useful having a partner who also was looking, but I can't say that any of our friends understood what we were looking for, because we already had so much. We had love; we had relative inner peace.

It wasn't that we were always focused on this search. In Mill Valley, I was focused on success as an acupuncturist, on getting enough clients, and the respect of my peers, and then finally, on taking care of my body as it burned out in exhaustion.

Maybe the burnout was the crux of it. Every time I would go far enough in a certain direction, I would burn out because I was going against myself, against some kind of silent, inner guidance. I could no longer live the lie I was living. This whole idea of "living the good life" burned away because that's just not it. I was actually not very smart. I kept running into walls, full speed ahead, and then falling flat on my back. Yet there was always something truly alive within me, searching for what was real.

I can't say I didn't get cynical. Before I met Papaji, I said to myself, "Even if I am to discover that the truth is non-existent, and this searching is all just a way of passing time, I need to find that out, too. Then I will be willing to live a life like most other people, and stop the crazy searching."

I was shocked that Papaji was the one who appeared as the teacher. I had said I wasn't interested in gurus or India. I had always believed that if I found a teacher, it would be in Japan, or someplace in nature, or it would be a woman. So it was quite beautiful and humbling just to experience Papaji's level of welcoming. He didn't care what my history was; he just saw directly into the yearning. He said, "Yes, you're in the right place."

When I look back, I can connect the dots. There is this mysterious mandala that either unfolds or it doesn't. It could just as easily not have happened that way. I almost didn't meet Eli because he wasn't the type of man I was looking for, so our coming together is also a miracle.

In the introduction of your book, you talk about how Papaji asked you to stop, to just be still. Did your so-called awakening happen in that one instant or were there steps along the way?

As I mentioned earlier, it was through that initial encounter with the psychologist that I first recognized there was something horrible inside that I was avoiding, a kind of energetic madness, an abyss of despair. I didn't expect my relationship with Papaji to lead me back into that. I had thought it would erase it. [She chuckles.]

In coming back to Maui after being with Papaji the first time, I was suddenly overcome with a sense of loss. I was no longer in that rarefied atmosphere, in love with my teacher. I had thoughts that I should never have gone to India and met him, because now I felt so horrible. It was at that point that I somehow remembered what he had said before I left: "Your assignment is to see what is still *here,* what is *always here.*" And that was the stopping. Prior to that, everything in me said, "Get away from this pain. This was all just a mistake, like a bad love affair. Get over it. Move on with your life."

Instead, I stopped fighting the horrible feelings. The despair felt yucky, familiar, and sickening, and under it was a dead, hopeless, existential nothingness. But finally, I wasn't doing anything in my mind to get away from it. I was just in it. In an instant, all of that fell away, and there I was in bliss, the same bliss I had been in at his feet, the same "in love," except that he wasn't around. Nothing had changed circumstantially. It was literally from one moment to the next. So, I had to see that the bliss arose not from getting away from anything, but just from being here and telling the truth.

I had prayed for a teacher. I trusted him. Forces were pulling on me emotionally, mentally, and circumstantially, but something was crossed in that moment. All of those pulls were suddenly more superficial than the deeper knowing. Of course there were other moments of revelation, and finally there was a pivotal moment that had nothing to do with going through anything difficult; it was just a clap of thunder.

Tell us about that thunderclap moment.

I don't know how to talk about it. I don't think I've ever been able to say anything satisfactory about it. It was really a split second of the erasure of doubt. Because even after being with Papaji, if a mood appeared, I assumed that the mood meant that I had lost whatever enlightenment I had gained when I was with Papaji, even though I saw the absurdity of that.

Finally, there was a profound relaxation and a willingness to discover the true meaning of vigilance. Vigilance is not a super-egoic task, an idea that I shouldn't be feeling this or thinking that, or that I should constantly be watching my thought. True vigilance is a much deeper level of recognizing yourself as pure awareness. I heard Papaji say that vigilance is required until your last breath.

When you talked about vigilance in satsang, *it challenged me to be more active.*

To me, vigilance is a holy word. It is to keep vigil as the light of awareness. In the past, I had interpreted vigilance as a kind of burden, like putting a lid on it, or making myself be a certain way. Vigilance is soft, open. In another sense, it is simply telling the truth.

There's a point where it's important to tell your story so that you can see where it is going. Then, you can begin to question, "Am I indulging this? Have I told this story too many times?" For me, it was an experience of internalizing Papaji, of giving myself *satsang*. If there was going to be an internal dialogue, it was going to be a dialogue of opening and seeing what is true, not the dialogue of collusion with fixation or suffering. Instead, my attention was turned toward true inquiry: "Who am I? What am I doing right now?"

If there is no inner dialogue, then nothing is needed, because there is nothing but spacious emptiness. If you are involved in your stories and an inner dialogue appears, it is useful to tell the truth about the quality of that dialogue. This is true vigilance. Not as something sanctimonious or preachy... definitely not. If it is preachy, there will be rebellion against it. Vigilance is simply an opening, a loving welcoming into truth.

Your invitation to meet the death of the self had a profound impact on me.

That's the stopping place. Death must be addressed. As organisms, we fear death. We're programmed to fear it. It's appropriate to fear death. That fear helps keep the body alive, and in that recognition, it's possible to also be willing to meet death. Death is why we fear stillness.

To meet death is to give up all possibility of making our relationships work better, or getting more enlightened, or getting healthier, whatever the latest "getting" is. When there *really* is no future possibility, this is death, and it is beautiful.

We think that letting go of these things will be horrible, because we perpetuate the hope that getting or perfecting will give us the beauty and peace we seek. In actuality, all beauty and peace are fully realized in the moment of giving up that hope, of giving up the future.

When I sat with that yesterday, I got up to this edge, this kind of precipice, and there was no going further.

That's OK. You can't go further by volition. All you can do is invite it and be willing. Even "trying to go further" is a distraction. It is a projection into the future. Just be open. Be willing. I don't advise "doing it" because "doing it" is a trick of the mind.

Ramana, my teacher's teacher, simply lay down on the floor and inquired into death. Obviously, when the body dies, there is no longer any breath, no longer any relations. He truly experienced this. His body even went into a kind of rigor mortis. What an awakening came from that!

Does this meeting death thing have to happen more than once? [We both laugh.]

Where does that question come from?

It probably sounds like I want to avoid this, but I'm really just curious about the process.

There are different kinds of deaths. Yes, smaller deaths may be met. The death of the body may be met. Finally, life itself must be met, and this is the true death.

Death has many faces. I would say that whatever face of death appears, it has to be met. If it's not possible to meet death as Ramana did, to meet the true absolute non-existence of this form, then smaller deaths can be met, such as the death of all attainment or all betterment. That in itself is the opening.

Was there a final point in time when the idea of a separate self was finished for you?

There was a point where the sense of me was done, absolutely, and then there was a point where the sense of me reappeared. It was gradual, but over time, I felt myself reincarnating. The sense of me was reappearing, and at first, I was terrified by it. I thought that meant something. Then I saw that it didn't make a difference. The sense of me is not separate from the truth of who I am. Then I really understood what my teacher had meant when he told me not to cling even to emptiness, because that is still an exclusion of form. It's all the same—nothingness, somethingness—all the same continuum.

It was necessary for this mind/body to recognize this, because there had been a clinging to emptiness, and an elevation of emptiness and the sense of no-me. It is a full circle. I returned to being a regular, ordinary woman. I am much more ordinary now than I have ever been.

Is there a different relationship with the sense of me now?

Oh yes! Before, it was a burden. Now, it is nothing. It is simply a sense, much like the body reappearing when you wake up in the morning.

You spoke earlier about relationship being an important teacher for you. Can you talk about your relationship with Eli?

Like all relationships, it goes through phases. Right now, we find ourselves once again in a honeymoon phase. So it's a really good time to be asking this question. [A little chuckle.]

We are both strong people. We have strong opinions. We are very different in the way we teach, but we both transmit the same message, because we both have the same teacher. As personalities, we are very different. He is a New York Jew, and I am Southern 50s WASP [White Anglo-Saxon Protestant]. He was a revolutionary, and I was trying to be normal. Our relationship is enriched by these differences. I love it. It reflects the possibility of people coming together and delighting in the differences, while discovering the essential sameness.

How is it different to be in relationship with Eli since your Self-realization?

In some ways, it is the same as it always was. We still have arguments. I say this is what happened, and he says, no, it didn't, it was like this, and then it can escalate. We are like every other couple.

Eli was my teacher initially. He knew that, and I knew that. I am a very good student, so at a certain point, I became his teacher. This is what a good student does, right? This lasted a few years, and then that form no longer worked. It doesn't work to be married to your student. It wasn't good for either one of us.

I realize now that I actually misused that time in certain ways. I was getting back at him a bit for when I was his student. [She laughs.] This was subconscious. I didn't fully know it. But then an even deeper relationship unfolded as husband and wife. There was still stuff leftover from old wars, from 30 years in a relationship that began when we were young and immature. There were things that had never gotten cleared up.

The idea of us facilitating a couples retreat had come up over the years, but we knew we couldn't do that. Not because we sometimes argue and fight, but because something still had to be seen regarding relationships.

In this last year, we actually broke up. [Editor's Note: It was later publicly disclosed that the cause of Gangaji and Eli's breakup was Eli's revealing to Gangaji that he had been involved in a three-year affair.]

We said, "This is the end of the marriage." A particular crisis arose that caused us to end our marriage, and then in that process we realized once again that we were deeply in love. There had been a middle ground where a very subtle war was going on. We agreed we didn't want this, and we cut each other free, which was major. We both felt enormous relief. Sadness at first, and then relief. How much easier not to be concerned! I knew we would be dearest, deepest friends. I loved him. I would love him for life. But I thought, "Thank God we don't have to be married anymore [she laughs]—we don't have to be in this relationship."

Through that freedom, we came back together in a different way. We were in Australia, and we had some time off together. We went through and deconstructed our whole relationship from the beginning, really looking at the resentments that had built up, that were left unspoken, or that we thought had disappeared. It was incredible. I had always been the one who was the tender of the relationship, but now he was ready to deconstruct our prior relationship and to be in a new relationship.

I've always known that relationship is the way for me, but Eli is very different. As a young person, he assumed that he would never have a relationship, his way was political, and he didn't want to be weighted down by relationship. So, from the beginning, there was ambivalence about the relationship.

I would say to him, "Why aren't you more fully here?" I know a lot of women feel this way. We know about being present because that is our gift. It was amazing for me to have to give this up. To recognize that relationship was *not* going to be the way that was to happen. To be released from that was beautiful.

It sounds like that release made it possible to come back together.

Yes, it was essential for us. We had never really ended it before. When something big would happen, neither one of us would let the other leave. In order to really tell the truth, we knew we had to end it, that it had gone as far as it could go like this. For us, this brought us back together. Other couples might not get back together.

We both feel coming back together like this is a miracle because we didn't expect it. We felt like it was time to end it, and that this was the right thing. Coming back together was a surprise. That's what I mean when I say we're in the honeymoon phase now. It is a mature honeymoon.

We realized that wow, we really did love each other relationally, not just as deep friends, but also as man and woman, and husband and wife, and as partners. We are each coming back whole, which 30 years ago would have been impossible. It doesn't mean that certain irritations don't appear, but the war is over. This is really what we are teaching about, how to end the war.

How do you see the feminine, how would you define it?

What's coming up for me now in our conversation is that the feminine is about relating. It's about connection, about humanness, about the Mother, about birth.

I've always known the feminine in Eli. He has a very deep, earthy, feminine side in him that I have always recognized. And he recognizes the masculine in me. I can have a very male energy, removed, analytical, cool even. We've always felt the "other" in each other. But when the chips are down, it turns out that there is more of a feminine energy here. It's what I have to offer as a body. This was actually a surprise.

I hadn't identified with the feminine in years because I had felt it to be a distraction for most people. Especially when I first started speaking, people would ask me to talk about the feminine, about the goddess, and I would say that it doesn't exist. Both male and female are completely made up. Forget about it. Ultimately, this is true; it is all the same essence, yet relationships have to do with polarities. This is what I mean about being more ordinary than ever because I do not reside in etheric realms of absolutes. I am fully back in the world.

In 1990, when you started teaching, you were one of the first teachers to come from Papaji, and you were certainly the first woman.

There had been other women teachers, some in the Buddhist tradition, such as Sharon Salzberg. But I don't think that there had ever been any so out in the public. I never say that I am enlightened. That's like declaring I am God. It's so open to misunderstanding. But I do say that I am fulfilled; my search is over.

When I first began teaching, to say this was outrageous. It was heresy—"Who do you think you are; you're supposed to be back in the trenches!" It's a declaration of the end of the war.

The challenges in the beginning were great. Papaji sent me out too soon, and this also was great. I had to get out there in the world and sink or swim. By making me a public figure, he gave me no room to indulge. Whatever was going on with me, there it was out in the open. The only direction Papaji had given me was to speak from my own experience. I had to ask myself if what I was saying was correct. I had to discover deeper and deeper if it was really the truth. It's not about understanding something conceptually. It's about direct experience.

Before all this, did you have a personality capable of handling such challenges?

No. Absolutely not. I couldn't handle anyone questioning or challenging me. I would crumple because I assumed they were right. I didn't know where to look to find what was right and what was wrong. I didn't know where to go inside to find reality. I was much more comfortable being a student than being a teacher.

I think this is relevant to your book, and to women and the feminine. It is time that we stand up and speak the truth of what we know. Women know a lot simply from what their bodies have gone through. We know a lot about meeting suffering, about what passes, what comes and goes. Women know an enormous amount about the broken heart and vulnerability. It's time for women to stand up. Not like men, but as ordinary women, telling the truth. There has been enough hiding.

Now what do you say when people ask you about the feminine?

It depends on the context, but it would probably all point to the same thing, which is that you absolutely must find what has no gender, what is before any principle of feminine or masculine.

Can you talk about the role of meditation?

Meditation can be useful to settle the mind, to let the mind quiet enough so that some peace can be experienced, some relative calm. This in itself is enormous support. But what often gets overlooked is what is being meditated on the rest of the day. What I usually direct people to discover is their primary meditation. Not those 30 minutes a day of sitting, but what is being meditated on once you get up from your cushion. This is where the real meditation is practiced. The usual, daily and hourly mediation is to follow thoughts. Yet, you can refuse to follow your thoughts. You don't need to stop them from happening, but you can be vigilant and refuse to follow them.

Is meditation critical to realizing our true nature?

No. It may help some people. It helped me enormously. But there is no formula for realization. There are people who have never meditated a single day and in one instant of realization, their life is never the same. It remains a mystery. I love meditation, but I also love exercise, and I recommend that people cook, garden, dance, and do what they like. It's whatever nourishes someone, and meditation can be deeply nourishing.

In satsang yesterday, someone asked how to make himself more available to silence, and you said something about paying attention to the process in which we make ourselves unavailable to silence.

Really what I'm saying is to stop trying to get anything. The only thing that arises in the stillness is the attempt to get something or to get away from something. When death is met, you are no longer trying to get anything else, and there is also no trying to get away from death, because you know it is going to get you anyway. When you stop running, the strategies also stop, and there is silence. Stillness is here. All mental activity is happening on the surface of stillness. It's not like you can get to it or reach it. It is *here*.

You travel all around the globe and you've been teaching for many years. What is your perspective on what's happening in the world?

Something is definitely happening. What it is, I can't be sure. We will see. Given the news of these times, and the fact that even mainstream science says that we are in trouble, that the poles are melting, etc., shakes people in deep, conscious and subconscious ways.

Who knows which way it's going to go? There could be a huge positive reaction, or the human capacity for denial could also crush any chance of the radical awakening needed. There could be an explosion of blossoming. It could be a time of the uprising of the human spirit. We are all a part of it. We cannot know the outcome, but we can know that our lives are contributing in some way to the outcome.

Catherine Ingram suggested that we can't be attached to the outcome.

Well, that's the secret. There's a way of both desiring a certain outcome and at the same time not being attached to it. Being attached to the outcome freezes your energy so that you actually can't contribute fully, effortlessly. Not being attached is a skillful means as well as a way of being happy.

What do you think your role is at this time?

To be true to myself. To speak when I must speak, and to be silent when I must be silent. And to wait and see. Everyone has a different role. Everyone can trust themselves at the deepest level. I'm not advising trusting thoughts or emotions, but what is deeper than what can be thought or felt, what is alive, and loves life, and wants to serve life. We can allow that innate intelligence to guide our lives to places of learning. Then our catastrophes, both personal and planetary, are for our learning.

Since you're one of the more well-known teachers, I have to ask, how have you managed the fame that comes with it?

At first, it was strange. You know, it's just so unreal. [Big laugh.] It's a projection. I understand this because I used to be star-struck with movie stars. Since then, I've met a few, and they are just people, as I am just a person. People who know me, whether they love me as a teacher or love me as a friend, know I'm just a person. This is the secret I *really* have to offer— that we all can just be people—and this is more extraordinary than any of us can know. There is something huge in just being truly human.

How do you spend your day? [We both laugh.]

Well, in the usual activities. I go to the grocery store. Lately, I've been enjoying cooking. I meet with groups. I'm getting ready to go on a retreat. I do regular things—take walks, go to movies, read books, do my work, answer letters. I'd say I have the perfect life, really. Look at my work. What luck! Can you imagine? I know you can too because look at your work.

We're all very lucky.

Anything final?

The crux of what I have to say is about telling the truth and trusting yourself. Tell the truth deeper and deeper, and trust yourself deeper and deeper. This is endless.

Endless?

Yes, I am still discovering it! Every opportunity, whether speaking to one another in groups, or just like this interview, there is always the possibility to tell the truth, to trust what comes out, and to see what is revealed.

෨෮෪

"Ordinary," I thought, as I walked away from Gangaji's house. I laughed at the obvious: those people that we imagine are the most extraordinary turn out to be ordinary; those who we imagine are the most ordinary surprise us by being extraordinary.

This realization deepened as I traveled back home. It is so easy to be that "awake animal" when in nature. But how about in an airport? I wondered how it would be to open up to the sights and sounds of this busy scene. While scooting along the moving walkway, I gave my full attention to the people going the opposite direction. All kinds of people—different shapes and faces and ages. I was deeply moved by the beauty and perfection of each unique expression. And I sensed in a way that words can't capture, the common thread that holds it all together.

It filled me with awe at the complexity of this world. And gratitude that somehow it all works. I became aware of how much my well-being depended upon each person to do their job with integrity—from the guy pumping gas into the airplane to the janitor cleaning the bathroom to the pilot at the helm. Ordinary people doing their jobs. All of this flashed through my mind as I moved along the walkway, tears in my eyes, and a smile on my face. Even here, in the midst of the hustle and bustle, there is complete perfection and beauty.

೫)ભ

A few weeks later, I had more trouble seeing the "perfection and beauty" when I learned that our land had been targeted for oil and gas drilling. Like so many people in the West, we don't own the mineral rights under our property, which means that there's a very real possibility that some big company could come in with huge trucks and derricks, drilling for 24 hours a day.

When I was telling Chris about it, I started to cry but he couldn't comfort me—he just got home from a long day at work and was feeling tired and overwhelmed. Before I knew it, I threw a bowl on the floor and walked away. It was strangely satisfying when it shattered into a hundred tiny pieces. The Goddess of Anger paying a visit (as Karen McPhee might say). But it didn't feel like very enlightened behavior!

Throughout my life—lovers leaving me, the end of friendships, even the grief of death—I have always had a place of refuge. Like the perfect mother, the mesa comforts in a way no human can, always available, always reliable, big enough to hold and dissolve all pain. So the idea of drilling rigs in my backyard was completely devastating.

Just before going to bed that night, I looked out the window at the moonlit landscape—not a single other light in view—only the snowy mountains on the horizon. Deep, dark silence. I thought about how things will change if they really do start drilling here. What will happen to this sanctuary? Suddenly, I heard Adya's voice: "Whatever your life preserver is, whatever you're hanging onto, will be challenged."

"Of course," I thought. "My relationship with the land is my personal life preserver. It couldn't be better orchestrated. Everything—and I mean *everything*—is perfect as it is. This threat is just another opportunity to surrender."

Looking out my window at the starry sky, I was reminded of that night so many years ago as a young girl seeing and experiencing the vastness for the first time. And I realized that the moon and stars, the whole universe, is a reflection of the great mystery *within me*. Though it's easier to experience this when gazing at the stars or walking in the woods, I suddenly knew that my experience of the mystery does not require being outdoors in nature. It is not separate from me—it is *who I am*. I fell asleep feeling deeply comforted and at peace.

When I woke up, I thought about what action I wanted to take about the oil and gas exploration. The peace I felt did not mean that I was going to just give up. But I also realized that there was no "enemy," no one to blame or resist—even the owners of the mineral rights. I saw them playing a role, just as I was playing a role. But at the core, it is not who we are. In fact, I had genuine respect for the person I needed to negotiate with. He was a nice guy doing his job, trying to protect the interests of Colorado's educational fund.

I knew that I had to let go of any attachment to the outcome, even if it meant there would be drilling on the mesa. Somehow I was able to dance in the center of these two opposites, caring about the land with all my heart but being OK with whatever happened. In the end, it was the man who worked for the State that was responsible for a brilliant compromise. Nope, he sure wasn't the enemy. And yes, of course, I was filled with relief when the documents were signed. The documents gave the homeowners, association a 70-year lease on the mineral rights.

CONCLUSION

EVEN THIS

After this incredible journey, traveling all over the country meeting wise women and experiencing their teachings, the reader may be wanting to know that I am now fulfilled and completely at peace. That's what the seeker would like to hear. Including what's left of the seeker in me. That's what a seeker does, tries to get from A to B, measuring progress along a linear path. But even though it is called the *direct path of awakening*, there is no path. Because truly, there is nowhere to go, no destination, nothing to seek.

So what does life look like as you begin to embody this teaching? I can only share my experience. To be honest, I am often identified with my body and emotions and thoughts. What's also true is that I know it's not who I *really* am. I am able to return to a place of rest and presence very quickly through a variety of ways. I can bring my attention to my senses. I can ask who is thinking this thought? And is it really true? I welcome whatever feeling is arising. I rarely get lost in the story, though there are times when it is harder to stay present. Like right now.

Just a few moments ago, as I am writing this conclusion, I got a call from Chris with the lab results of the biopsy from last week. The lump in his jaw is lymphoma. At this moment, I don't know a lot about what that means but I do know it is cancer. Cancer is scary. Cancer is the unknown. Cancer can mean death.

All week while waiting for the results, I found myself in tears, realizing how fragile, how precious this life is. And there is also the story: "Oh no. I just can't go through this again—the stress, the pain, the unknown. The fear of losing my partner. Not again. And what are we going to do without health insurance, how will we pay for all the treatments, how will we manage?!"

But it doesn't last long because I catch myself quickly now. I know I am not being present when I start thinking about the future. No drama, no projecting into the "what-ifs." Just what is happening right now? Sadness, yes. Fear of being alone, yes. And once more, the recurring theme: facing the awesome reality of death. So I turn to the feelings and welcome them.

After a few tears, I wonder if I will be able to see the perfection and beauty in this, even this. A diagnosis of cancer. Yes. I am already letting this in. It is what is. There's no sense arguing with reality.

Adyashanti says that enlightenment is accepting what is. He also says that resistance is futile. It really is so simple. Not easy sometimes, but simple. And I embrace this mystery, this blessed life, *all* of it. Yes. Even this. Even this.

AFTERWORD

It is months since I wrote the last chapter. It will be months before these words are in your hands. That's the nature of writing, it's a snapshot of a passing moment in time. More than one of the women in the book has commented about how much has changed since our interviews: changes externally in one's circumstances and internally as the knowing deepens. At the same time, there is much that has not changed. Truth is eternal.

The biggest change for me is that Chris has completed six months of chemotherapy and is cancer-free. As his hair returns, so does his energy and vitality. It is a relief and a blessing. All is well.

CONTACT DETAILS

Rita Marie Robinson
www.extraordinarywisdom.net

Pamela Wilson
www.pamelasatsang.com

Sharon Landrith
www.clearlightsangha.org

Chameli Gad Ardagh
www.wildlove.org
www.livingessence.com

Muni Fluss
www.meetingwithmuni.com

Dorothy Hunt
www.dorothyhunt.org

Marlies Cocheret de la Morinière
www.marliescocheret.com

Karen McPhee
www.karenmcphee.com

Annette Knopp

www.thefreeheart.com

Francie Halderman

www.franciesatsang.com

Neelam

www.neelam.org

Catherine Ingram

www.dharmadialogues.org

Gangaji

www.gangaji.org

MORE ORDINARY WOMEN WITH EXTRAORDINARY WISDOM

This "waking-up" is happening all over the country, the world, and right in our backyard. Here are a few more examples of this growing phenomenon, women whom I met and for various reasons, could not be included in the book.

Joi Sharp is a disciple of Mata Amritatandamayi (Ammachi). She spent nine years living with Amma in her ashram in South India. With Amma's blessing she then lived for two years at Ramana Maharshi's ashram. Joi was invited to start giving *satsang* by Pamela Wilson and with Amma's instruction, she offers weekly *satsang* in her town of Ridgway, Colorado.

www.satsangwithjoi.com

Meike Schuett recognized the truth of being in 1998 as she entered the room where Isaac Shapiro was offering *satsang*. Since then her life has been a celebration of the love affair with *now*. Originally from Germany, she now lives in Byron Bay, Australia when not traveling the world with Isaac, offering Meetings in Truth. She is available to all who are interested.

www.isaacshapiro.de

Moni Vangolen offers unraveling services to individuals and groups. Her carefully knitted illusory self was unraveled with the guidance provided by two enlightened masters, one being Eckhart Tolle. Her gatherings—Meetings in Stillness—are devoted to spiritual realization—being our true Self. While grounded in Eckhart's teachings from the many years spent closely in his presence and with his blessing, Moni teaches from direct experience of realization and what it is to embody and live this presence. Recently she teamed up with her partner, Tomas Stubbs, who had been sharing the truth in Europe when they met. They delight in holding meetings together in Vancouver where they live and in other parts of Canada, USA, UK, France and Spain.

www.livingpresence.ca

Jeannie Zandi is a consultant, retreat leader, counselor, writer, poet and mother whose passion is the recognition of our deepest being and its embodiment, which she calls *Living as Love*. She holds an M.A. from Naropa University in Transpersonal Counseling Psychology. Jeannie leads groups, retreats and works with people privately to support the unfolding of Love in everyday life, work, and play. She mediates, sings to, teases and flirts with the Divine in each for no other reason than it's her nature and joy. Jeannie is available locally in Taos and in various locations around the country.

www.jeanniezandi.com

FURTHER READING

The following are some of the books that I personally found most helpful in understanding the direct path of awakening. There are many, many more—you can go online and search for non-dual teachings or non-duality.

Adyashanti, *The Impact of Awakening: Excerpts from the Teachings of Adyashanti*, Open Gate, Los Gatos, California, 2000
 —*Emptiness Dancing: Selected Dharma Talks of Adyashanti*, Sounds True, Boulder, Colorado, 2006
Ardagh, Arjuna, *The Translucent Revolution: How People Just Like You Are Waking Up and Changing the World*, New World Library, Novato, California, 2005
Gangaji, *Diamond in Your Pocket*, Sounds True, Boulder, Colorado, 2005
Hunt, Dorothy, *Only This!*, San Francisco Center for Meditation and Psychotherapy, San Francisco, California, 2004
Ingram, Catherine, *Passionate Presence*, Gotham, New York, 2003
Katie, Byron, with Stephen Mitchell, *Loving What Is: Four Questions That Can Change Your Life*, Three Rivers Press, New York, 2002
 —*A Thousand Names for Joy: Living in Harmony with the Way Things Are*, Harmony, New York, 2007
Marvelly, Paula, *The Teachers of One: Living Advaita: Conversations on the Nature of Non-Duality*, Watkins Publishing, London, 2002
Tolle, Eckhart, *The Power of Now*, New World Library, Novato, California, 1999
 —*A New Earth: Awakening to Your Life's Purpose*, Dutton Adult, New York, 2005

O

is a symbol of the world,
of oneness and unity. O Books
explores the many paths of wholeness
and spiritual understanding which
different traditions have developed down
the ages. It aims to bring this knowledge
in accessible form, to a general readership,
providing practical spirituality to today's seekers.

For the full list of over 200 titles covering:

- CHILDREN'S PRAYER, NOVELTY AND GIFT BOOKS
- CHILDREN'S CHRISTIAN AND SPIRITUALITY
- CHRISTMAS AND EASTER
- RELIGION/PHILOSOPHY
- SCHOOL TITLES
- ANGELS/CHANNELLING
- HEALING/MEDITATION
- SELF-HELP/RELATIONSHIPS
- ASTROLOGY/NUMEROLOGY
- SPIRITUAL ENQUIRY
- CHRISTIANITY, EVANGELICAL
  AND LIBERAL/RADICAL
- CURRENT AFFAIRS
- HISTORY/BIOGRAPHY
- INSPIRATIONAL/DEVOTIONAL
- WORLD RELIGIONS/INTERFAITH
- BIOGRAPHY AND FICTION
- BIBLE AND REFERENCE
- SCIENCE/PSYCHOLOGY

Please visit our website,
www.O-books.net

Back to the Truth
5,000 years of Advaita
Dennis Waite

A wonderful book. Encyclopedic in nature, and destined to become a classic. **James Braha**
Absolutely brilliant...an ease of writing with a water-tight argument outlining the great universal truths. This book will become a modern classic. A milestone in the history of Advaita. **Paula Marvelly**
1905047614 500pp **£19.95 $29.95**

The Book of One
The spiritual path of Advaita
Dennis Waite

3rd printing
A magisterial survey that belongs on the shelves of any serious student. **Scientific and Medical Network Review**
1903816416 288pp **£9.99 $17.95**

Everything is a Blessing
Make your life a little easier, less stressful and more meaningful
David Vennells

I've read a few self-help books in my time, but this is the only one I've ever talked about with no reserve or irony. Vennells charmed me

utterly with his open enthusiasm, simple presentations of deep spiritual truths, suggestions for achievable goals and workable plans and doable exercises. **Marion Allan Reviews**
1905047223 160pp **£11.99 $19.95**

How to Meet Yourself
...and find true happiness
Dennis Waite

A comprehensive survey of the psychological and philosophical dynamics of the human condition, offering an everlasting solution to discovering true happiness in the moment. I highly recommend it. Dennis Waite is one of the foremost contemporary writers on Advaita Vedanta in the West. **Paula Marvelly**, author of The Teachers of One.
1846940419 260pp **£11.99 $24.95**

The Jain Path: Ancient Wisdom for the West
Aidan Rankin

The best introduction to Jainism available. It is at once very topical, clear and engaging. **David Frawley** (Pandit Vamdeva Shastri), Director of the American Institute of Vedic Studies.
A book that is full of wisdom and intelligence. **William Bloom**, Director of The Holism Network
1905047215 240pp **£11.99 $22.95**

One Self
Life as a means of transformation
Philip Jacobs

This is a compelling and life enhancing book for anyone having to face a long term illness, but also so wise that it can help any of us to understand our path in life even if we are not so severely challenged.
Peter Fenwick, Scientific and Medical Network
1905047673 160pp **£9.99 $19.95**

The Supreme Self
The way to enlightenment
S. Abhayananda

A wonderful synopsis of mystical religions and their numinous goals. Swami Abhayananda is a true teacher. **Jack Haas**, author of *The Way of Wonder*
I can think of no better book to put in the hands of the serious spiritual seeker. **Amazon**
1905047452 224pp **£10.99 $19.95**

The Wisdom of Vedanta
An introduction to the philosophy of non-dualism
S. Abhayananda

Vedanta is the philosophy of Self-realization, which had its origin in the Upanishads of ancient India, and which lives today as the timeless yet ever-new wisdom known as "the perennial philosophy." This is one of the best introductions available.
1905047509 272pp **£11.99 $24.95**

The Bhagavad Gita
Alan Jacobs

Alan Jacobs has succeeded in revitalising the ancient text of the Bhagavad Gita into a form which reveals the full majesty of this magnificent Hindu scripture, as well as its practical message for today's seekers. His incisive philosophic commentary dusts off all the archaism of 1500 years and restores the text as a transforming instrument pointing the way to Self Realization. **Cygnus Review**
1903816513 320pp £12.99 $19.95

Everyday Buddha
A contemporary rendering of the Buddhist classic, the Dhammapada
Karma Yonten Senge (Lawrence Ellyard)
Foreword by His Holiness the 14th Dalai Lama

Excellent. Whether you already have a copy of the Dhammapada or not, I recommend you get this. I congratulate all involved in this project and have put the book on my recommended list. **Jeremy Ball**
Nova Magazine
1905047304 144pp **£9.99 $19.95**

Good As New
A radical retelling of the scriptures
John Henson

An immensely valuable addition to scriptural understanding and appreciation. **Methodist Recorder**
A short review cannot begin to persuade readers of the value of this book. Buy it and read it. But only if you are brave enough. Renew

2nd printing in hardback
1903816734 448pp **£19.99 $24.95** cl
1905047118 448pp **£11.99 $19.95** pb

The Ocean of Wisdom
The most comprehensive compendium of worldly and spiritual wisdom this century
Alan Jacobs

This anthology of 5,000 passages of spiritual wisdom is an awesome collection of prose and poetry, offering profound truths to everyday guidance. A valuable reference for any writer or historian, but it also makes for a good fireside or bedside book. **Academy of Religion and Psychical Research**
190504707X 744pp 230/153mm **£17.99 $29.95**

Popol Vuh: The Sacred Book of the Maya
The Mayan creation story
Allen J. Christenson

The most accurate and comprehensive translation ever produced. His work is an extraordinary masterpiece of scholarly analysis.
Karen Bassie-Sweet, University of Calgary.
Clear, vital and entrancingly true...a brilliant exegesis, worthy of the treasure it unpacks. **David Freidel**, Southern Methodist University
190381653X 320pp 230/153mm **£19.99 $29.95**

Popol Vuh II
A literal, line by line translation
Allen J. Christenson

A definitive document of rhetorical brilliance. **Stephen Houston,** Jesse Knight University Professor, Brigham Young Univ.
An invaluable contribution... **Justin Kerr,** author of *The Maya Vase* books.
1903816572 280pp 230/153mm **£25.00 $37.50**

The Principal Upanishads
Alan Jacobs

Alan Jacobs has produced yet another literary masterpiece in his transcreation of the 'Principal Upanishads', which together with his 'Bhagavad Gita', aim to convey the nondualist teaching (Advaita Vedanta) of the ancient Indian scriptures as well as explore the author's own poetic expression. **Paula Marvelly**
1903816505 384pp **£12.99 $19.95**

The Spiritual Wisdom of Marcus Aurelius
Practical philosophy from an ancient master
Alan Jacobs

Most translations are literal and arid but Jacobs has paraphrased a selection of the best of Aurelius' meditations so as to give more force to the essential truths of his philosophy. **The Light**
There's an uncanny appropriateness of this work to current times so this book is bound to resonate with many. **Wave**
1903816742 260pp **£9.99 $14.95**

A World Religions Bible
Robert van de Weyer

An admirable book to own personally for reflection and meditation, with the possibility of contemplating a different extract a day over an entire year. It is our hope that the use of this splendid anthology will grow. We recommend it to all for their personal enrichment. **The Friend**
Outstanding collection of religious wisdom...never has so much wisdom been concentrated in such a small space. **New Age Retailer**
1903816157 432pp full colour throughout 180/120mm **£19.99 $28.95**

A Heart for the World
The interfaith alternative
Marcus Braybrooke

This book is really needed. This is the blueprint. It has to be cherished. Faith in Jesus is not about creeds or homilies. It is a willingness to imitate Christ-as the Hindu guru Gandhi did so well. A must book to buy. **Peacelinks, IFOR**
1905047436 168pp **£12.99 $24.95**

Bringing God Back to Earth
John Hunt

Knowledgeable in theology, philosophy, science and history. Time and again it is remarkable how he brings the important issues into relation with one another... thought provoking in almost every sentence, difficult to put down. **Faith and Freedom**

An absorbing and highly readable book, profound and wide ranging.
The Unitarian
1903816815 320pp **£9.99 $14.95**

Christ Across the Ganges
Hindu responses to Jesus
Sandy Bharat

This is a fascinating and wide-ranging overview of a subject of great importance. It is a must for anyone interested in the history of religious traditions and in the interaction between faiths. **Marianne Rankin**, Alister Hardy Society
1846940001 224pp 230/153mm 6x9 **£14.99 $29.95**

A Global Guide to Interfaith
Reflections from around the world
Sandy and Jael Bharat

For those who are new to interfaith this amazing book will give a wonderful picture of the variety and excitement of this journey of discovery. It tells us something about the world religions, about interfaith history and organizations, how to plan an interfaith meeting and much more - mostly through the words of practitioners.
Marcus Braybrooke
1905047975 336pp 230/153mm 6x9 **£19.99 $34.95**

The Hindu Christ
Jesus' message through Eastern eyes
John Martin Sahajananda

To the conventional theologian steeped in the Judaeo-Christian tradition, this book is challenging and may even be shocking at times. For mature Christians and thinkers from other faiths, it makes its contribution to an emerging Christian theology from the East that brings in a new perspective to Christian thought and vision.
Westminster Interfaith
190504755X 128pp **£9.99 $19.95**

The History of Now
A guide to higher yearnings
Andy Nathan

This is all about the spark of optimism that gets us out of bed in the morning, and the different ways it has flared to life during the time of humanity. A "who's who" of the world religions.
1903816289 160pp 250/153mm **£9.99**

Islam and the West
Robert van de Weyer
2nd printing

Argues that though in the sphere of economics and politics relationships between Islam and the West have often been hostile, in the area of ideas and philosophy the two have much in common, indeed are interdependent.

A military and financial jihad against global terrorism cannot be won. Bit a jihad for peace can, and will render the first jihad unnecessary.

1903816149 128pp **£6.99**

Trading Faith
Global religion in an age of rapid change
David Hart

Argues boldly that the metaphor of trading provides the most useful model for religious exchanges in a world of rapid change. It is the inspiring biography of an intensely spiritual man with a great sense of humour who has chosen an unusual and courageous religious path. **Dr Anna King**, Lecturer in Hinduism, University of Winchester

1905047967 260pp **£10.99 $24.95**

Transcending Terror
A history of our spiritual quest and the challenge of the new millennium
Ian Hackett

Looks at the history of the major world religions, paying particular to nine great prophets, their teachings and what later generations have made of them. All are presented as stemming from the human quest for truth in every age. A return to the core values of all our faiths, putting aside partisanship and the desire to dominate is the only sure way forward, in order to "allow both our human and spiritual quests to continue as one family sharing one world." **Westminster Interfaith**

190381674 320pp **£12.99 $19.95**

You Are the Light
Rediscovering the Eastern Jesus
John Martin Shajananda
2nd printing

Closed systems, structures and beliefs have prevailed over the last 2000 years, cutting off the majority from direct contact with God and sharing Jesus's own insight on non-duality. This is an inspiring new contemplative vision. **Scientific and Medical Network Review**
1903816300 224pp **£9.99 $15.95**

Punk Science
Inside the mind of God
Manjir Samanta-Laughton

Wow! Punk Science is an extraordinary journey from the microcosm of the atom to the macrocosm of the Universe and all stops in between. Manjir Samanta-Laughton's synthesis of cosmology and consciousness is sheer genius. It is elegant, simple and, as an added bonus, makes great reading. **Dr Bruce H. Lipton**, author of *The Biology of Belief*
1905047932 320pp **£12.95 $22.95**

Mysticism and Science
A call to reconciliation
S. Abhayananda

A lucid and inspiring contribution to the great philosophical task of our age - the marriage of the perennial gnosis with modern science.
Timothy Freke author of *The Jesus Mysteries*

184694032X 144pp **£9.99 $19.95**

The Science of Oneness
A world view for the twenty-first century
Malcolm Hollick

A comprehensive and multi-faceted guide to the emerging world view. Malcolm Hollick brilliantly guides the reader intellectually and intuitively through the varied terrains of the sciences, psychology, philosophy and religion and builds up a vibrant picture that amounts to a new vision of reality for the 21st century. A veritable tour de force. **David Lorimer**, Programme Director, Scientific and Medical Network
1905047711 464pp 230/153mm **£14.99 $29.95**

The Wave
A life-changing insight into the heart and mind of the cosmos
Jude Currivan
2nd printing

Rarely does a book as fine as The Wave come along - this is a true treasure trove of ancient and current learning, covering a wide variety of interests. Accessible, interesting, educational and inspiring. The reader will find that both the intellect and the heart are gratified with this book, and that on a deeper level, much of it feels right - and that may be the best kind of knowledge. **Merlian News**
1905047339 320pp **£11.99 $19.95**